STEPHANIE PETERSEN

FRONT TABLE BOOKS
AN IMPRINT OF CEDAR FORT, INC
SPRINGVILLE, UTAH

ISBN 13: 978-1-4621-1295-1

Published by Front Table Books, an imprint of Cedar Fort, Inc.
2373 W. 700 S., Springville, UT 84663
Distributed by Cedar Fort, Inc., www.cedarfort.com

Library of Congress Cataloging-in-Publication Data on file

Cover and page design by Erica Dixon
Cover design © 2014 by Lyle Mortimer

Printed in China

10 9 8 7 6 5 4 3 2 1

To the Bread of Life that has given me so much peace.

To darling children who tolerated a creative mother
making roses while they made monsters out of play dough.

To a mother who taught me to draw on blank paper and make my own art.

To a father who gave me an eye for color and nature.

CONTENTS

INTRODUCTION

Bread has always been an integral part of my existence. I can think back on many happy moments at my mother's kitchen table as I gingerly rolled around a ball of dough while playing in the freshly milled, nutty smelling whole grain flour. If I think about bread too much, I almost cry with all the memories of love that it invokes. Bread for me is the embodiment of all the nurturing and joy that I've ever had in my life, and it is because of this fondness for the art of bread baking that I first started the study of bread professionally. It wasn't until I was several years into my experience as a professional baker that I realized what a blessing bread baking truly was to me. After a long week of work, I would often find myself in the kitchen at home baking again. This time instead of baking being the work of the day, it became the relaxation and meditation of my soul. I found that, without fail, when everything else in my life was a little too chaotic, bread was always grounding. It always had a slow and calming rhythm. Kneading the loaves was meditative, exacting, and artistic. It connected me to my creative soul and, by so doing, gave me the power to move forward with my life. Bread baking infused me with renewed zeal. It will do the same for you.

Bread baking, to my dismay, is becoming a completely lost art. Julia Child once said, "How can a nation be great when its bread tastes like Kleenex?" I'm a bit of an idealist. I know it. Gone are the days when mothers or grandmothers gather their children together to bake bread. Fathers who bake bread with their children are few and far between. I rarely see such a man. I hope to bring those days of bread baking back. I hope that by writing this book, I will inspire you to spend a little more time creating beauty.

I also realize we live in a busy world—if you never bake bread, you can still employ many of the bread-decorating techniques used in this book to add embellishments to prebaked loaves purchased from your local bakery!

I hope to inspire nurturing and expression within your home and your heart. Many of life's greatest lessons of love and peace can be taught over a loaf of freshly made (or decorated) bread. I hope to simplify the process enough that, even in a busy world, you feel you can make bread a priority. If I only reach one amazing, new creative genius with this book, I hope it is your genius.

What you are holding in your hands is a starting point for your own bread-baking journey. If you're a seasoned baker, this is a remarkable reference for a form of bread baking you may have never experienced. If you are a new baker, this book will give you all that you need to become a breadmaker. If you are an artist looking for a new medium, this book will be an excellent resource for a new form of art! Beautiful artistic bread is easy to make, and I hope that you will want to come back to the kitchen time and time again. Get out your flour. Find your apron. It's time to once again create joy. Onward and upward we go!

Stephanie Petersen

THE BASICS OF GOOD DOUGH FORMATION

FLOUR

The basic composition of the flour you use to make your bread dough will vary in protein content, depending on what kind of bread you are making. In this book, I use a variety of flours—not all flour is the same in terms of how it will bake and how it will act when manipulated and sculpted. For the base of your breads—meaning the main body of the loaf—I will often refer to the use of bread flour or high-protein flours. This is because the protein needed to form magnificent bread must be high enough for the gas that is produced during the fermentation process to be captured in the bread. This is often what will set apart a beautifully shaped loaf from a flat or squatty loaf.

SPECIALTY FLOUR

The decorative bread used throughout this book is generally based with part all-purpose wheat flour and part rye or oat flour. The addition of the rye or oat flour will make for lower protein content. The shape of the decorative embellishments will be retained during baking when this lower protein flour is used. Some of the decorative dough is sweetened or flavored. You'll find the one you prefer in your personal baking.

SWEETENERS

Notice as you study the recipes throughout this book that some of the bread is sweet dough while others are less sweet and can be used for savory applications. I've tried as much as possible to make sure that the flavors will be complementary in each loaf. You'll find that your personal taste may require more or less sweetness. In most cases I tend to under-sweeten my loaves. Adding additional sugar may slow down how quickly the yeast works, which sounds crazy; though yeast "eats" sugar, it will not do well with a large addition of sugar. Stick to the recipe as closely as possible.

YEAST

Yeast is a single-celled organism that feeds on sugar and, by so doing, expels carbon dioxide gas and alcohol. The process by which it works in conjunction with sugars and liquid is called *fermentation.* In most cases I prefer a long and slow fermentation with much lower yeast content in the dough than most standard recipes. This will give you the most complex and delightful texture and flavor. Adding more yeast will generally cause your bread to be coarse and have a less-refined characteristic. Of all the ingredients in breadmaking, the one most integral in its measurement is yeast. Use measuring spoons and tools that are designed for baking and not for the dinner table. When I refer to a specific measurement in a recipe, it is because I know that that measurement will work.

WHEN WORKING WITH YEAST, HERE ARE A FEW THINGS TO REMEMBER:

- Because yeast is a living organism, always use lukewarm water (less than 110°F) to active the yeast. Higher temperatures will usually kill the yeast and your bread will not rise.
- When yeast is active, never add salt directly to the water and yeast combination because it greatly inhibits yeast activity and can potentially kill the yeast. To keep this from happening, I always combine the salt with the flour.
- If you use a stronger yeast, such as a SAF or bread machine yeast, you will need less yeast in recipes. These super yeasts will cause the bread to rise about 30 percent faster than standard active dry yeast.
- As a general rule, use about half the amount of yeast you would use in a regular recipe if you are living over 3000 feet above sea level. Higher altitude baking requires less yeast to achieve success.
- Allow your dough to rise at a medium temperature, no higher than 85–90°F. This will allow the yeast to work at its optimum. Some recipes specify to raise the bread at room temperature, while others are put in the fridge to slow down the fermentation of the dough. If you keep your home cold or live in a colder climate, the bread will rise slower and may need to be put in a slightly warmed oven. I don't recommend putting loaves in the oven often or for the full amount of time since this method generally results in an overly yeasty flavor in the bread.

SALT

Salt is not merely for added flavor enhancement in bread, though it does that job rather well. Salt has a natural ability to kill bacteria and organisms when it comes in contact with them. The small quantity of salt used in conjunction with the yeast in these bread recipes is designed to help regulate how quickly the bread will rise as well as how outstanding the bread will taste. If you need low-sodium bread, you may use a natural sea salt or potassium chloride in place of the regular salt. The flavor will remain the same, and you should still have a fairly well-regulated fermentation time.

SHORTENING

Any fat that I use will shorten the connection of the proteins in the dough. The addition of fat to dough is generally for two purposes: First, for added tenderness to the finished product you bake. The fat will help the dough remain moist even a few days after baking. Second, fat will help to condition the proteins in the dough, adding to the elasticity of the loaf. Fat is not always necessary in the base loaves, but will be necessary for the decorative embellishment dough on top of your loaves.

GENERAL BREAD TIPS

GLUTEN FORMATION

Gluten is the naturally occurring protein in all wheat flours. Soft wheat will produce a cake or low-protein flour. Hard wheat will produce a high-protein or bread flour. If you are not milling your own flour, look for high-protein flour to make your bread. The connection of the gluten proteins in your bread will be a pivotal part of great structure in your loaf. When wheat protein comes in contact with liquid, the proteins will connect in a sponge-like structure. Kneading bread will generally connect the gluten strands in such a way that the bread will look and taste wonderful.

TEMPERATURES

In all recipes that use yeast, be particularly aware of how hot the liquid is when adding it to the dry ingredients. Yeast should not come in contact with liquid that is much hotter than 110 degrees. As a general rule, I keep my liquid at body temperature or lower. Also, I generally allow my dough to ferment at temperatures between 85 and 90 degrees. This median temperature ensures a good flavor in the bread. Higher-temperature fermentation can cause the dough to taste overly yeasty or become sour.

Baking temperatures refer to a preheated oven. If you do not preheat your oven, the yeast will not be killed soon enough in the baking process. This usually results in dough bulging out of the side structure of your loaves, which will have adverse aesthetic appeal. The bread will still be fine to eat, but it will not look as beautiful as you would expect.

Cool loaves on a rack before storing them or wrapping them with plastic. This will prevent the loaves from coming in contact with condensation inside the wrapping, which would cause the bread to become soggy.

FLAVOR

The flavor of perfect bread is distinct. One should experience the taste of the nutty fresh wheat if whole grain loaves are made. That milder taste should be well pronounced and not accentuated with anything too salty, bitter, sour, or yeasty. When you taste good bread, you should be impressed immediately by the depth of the flavor of the grain. The only exception to this would be the addition of herbs, nuts, fruit, or spices. Even then, flavor additions should bring harmonious notes to your loaf, not an overpowering dominion of taste. Keep this in mind and you will find that your loaves are well received by everyone who has the chance to break through your fresh-baked crust.

MEASURING TOOLS

Professional bakers use scales and weights for their breadmaking. Every ingredient is carefully put on the scale and measured. I refer to the use of a scale only a few times in this book because it can sometimes be intimidating to a novice baker. Instead, I have geared these recipes toward the home baker. If the use of a scale is needed, I will specify.

Remember when measuring flour to lightly scoop the flour into a kitchen measuring cup intended for dry measurements. A coffee cup isn't a measuring cup. You need to invest in standard measuring cups.

For liquid measurements, use a graduated measuring cup (they are usually glass with a small spout on one side). These are made for accuracy in reading liquid measurements.

Pay close attention to the amount of yeast to use and always flatten the top of the ingredients in the measuring spoon. Using a rounded measurement is not accurate.

In most cases, I raise my bread in a flat-sided crock or food-grade bucket. These make measuring when the dough has doubled easier, which will ensure proper development and structure in the bread.

I will ask you only a few times to weigh the dough when making a loaf or roll. Though this method is preferred in bake shops, it isn't always necessary when working in smaller numbers at home. Again, this book was written for home bakers.

YEAST ADJUSTMENT SCHEDULE

Do you want to make bread fit into your busy schedule? The following is a tool (one of my favorite things ever) that will help you gauge the amount of yeast to add to dough to adjust the time in which it will be ready to bake. All measurements are as accurate as I could make them. Please be advised it may take a few tries to get the exact amount you want for your life. This will be applied directly to my Basic Whole Wheat Bread recipe (p. 28). It can be adjusted for the five-day bread dough as well (p. 21)—just double the amount of active dry yeast (since that recipe makes about double the amount of bread as the basic bread recipe). Be very accurate in your yeast measurements and don't use the quick-rise yeast (unless the recipe specifies to do so). Never skimp on the fermentation process. You'll find that the longer and slower the bread rises, the more beautiful and full of depth the flavor of your bread. Let bread fit in *your* schedule. It should be a part of life that you can control.

BREAD SCHEDULE ADJUSTMENT FOR YEAST QUANTITY AND TEMPERATURE

In these adjustments, temperature is the most critical variable! If you can keep your dough within five degrees of what you intended, you can time it very closely to be ready when you want.

If you use your fridge for the rise, warm the dough to room temperature before baking.

Also, seal the container and flatten the dough as much as you can so the temperature is even. Dough kneaded by machine (in slow, long rises) needs cooler liquid added to the dough during mixing instead of warm liquid. The friction of the mixer will already add warmth to the dough.

Unless you live in a cold climate, I don't recommend using the oven as a tool for proofing (raising) your bread—controlling the temperature in most standard ovens is difficult. Unless you have a digital oven that lets you program the exact temperature in your oven, don't put bread in the oven until it is ready to bake.

Invest in a chef-style meat thermometer with a metal stick. They are only a few dollars but make a big difference in your baking experience. A meat thermometer is where the science comes into breadmaking. You'll be able to see the exact internal temperature of your dough. I also use a meat thermometer when I start working with the decorative dough embellishments.

After the first rise (especially with dough raised under refrigeration), dough should be warmed to room temperature. Check the temperatures!

I have factored into the time needed the fact that mixing by hand will take ten to fifteen minutes.

Baking is constant for all doughs, except for the sweet variations. For a standard-sized sandwich loaf: 425°F for 15 minutes, then lower the oven temperature to 350°F for 30–40 minutes

YEAST ADJUSTMENT SCHEDULE

DOUGH TYPE	ACTIVE DRY YEAST	DOUGH TEMPERATURE	FIRST RISE	SHAPE/PROOF
FAST RISE	4 tsp.	80–90°F	1 h. 30 min.	45 min.
NORMAL RISE	2 tsp.	70–80°F	2 h. 15 min.	1 h.
LONG NORMAL RISE	2 tsp.	65–70°F	4 h. 30 min	1 h. 30 min.
12-HOUR RISE	½ tsp.	70°F	8–10 h.	3–4 h.
16-HOUR RISE	½ tsp.	55–60°F	8–10 h.	8 h (2 h. at 90°F)
24-HOUR RISE	¼ tsp.	40–55°F	Deflate every 8 h.	2 h. 30 min. at 90°F

SIMPLE BREAD RECIPES

The base for any decorative loaf

NO-KNEAD FOUR-INGREDIENT BREAD

1 standard-sized loaf or 12 medium-sized dinner rolls

3½ cups unbleached bread flour

2 tsp. salt

¼ tsp. instant SAF yeast (or ½ tsp. active dry yeast)

1¼–1½ cups water (under 110°F)

This basic bread doesn't require any kneading or special bread-baking experience. It makes a single loaf. Remember to measure your ingredients exactly. I don't use a scale to measure the weight of the ingredients in this recipe. Remember not to pack the flour into the measuring cups; instead, lightly fill the cups with flour and level off the measuring cup using the flat side of a knife. This will ensure that the recipe turns out well. I use instant SAF yeast. This yeast is 30 percent stronger than regular active yeast. It can be found in the baking aisle of most grocery stores, labeled bread machine *yeast. If the amount of yeast in this recipe seems low, keep in mind that it has a long, slow rise and fermentation. This longer time will allow the dough to basically knead itself and for the yeast to change the structure of the proteins in the dough. Adding more yeast than the recipe calls for will not give you a better loaf of bread. In fact, using more yeast in this case will make the bread taste overly yeasty.*

DIRECTIONS:

1. Combine the ingredients in a 1-gallon food-grade bucket (or a 1-gallon bowl with a lid) until everything is mixed and smooth. Combining everything takes 20–30 turns by hand. You may need more water, depending on how dry your flour is and the conditions of flour storage.

DIRECTIONS CONTINUED ON NEXT PAGE

2. Cover with a lid and keep covered at room temperature until you're ready to bake bread, 10–12 hours.

BAKING A LOAF:

Form dough into a loaf and place on a lightly oiled baking stone or in a greased 8-inch loaf pan. Allow to rise in a warm room until doubled, about 2 hours. Bake at 375°F for 35–40 minutes (meat thermometer will register 165°F or more). Enjoy!

BAKING DINNER ROLLS:

Divide dough into 12 rolls and form according to the roll-molding tips on page 68. Place on a lightly greased baking sheet, 2 inches apart, and allow to rise until doubled, 2–2½ hours. Lightly mist with water and bake in a preheated 425-degree oven for 20–25 minutes.

CHEF'S NOTES:

A few factors can have an effect on the lightness of this bread:

- TEMPERATURE: *Raising the bread during the winter months will take up to 1 hour longer for the second rise in the pan. I keep it around 70 degrees in the house during the winter. A good 10 degrees colder inside will make a difference in how fast the bread rises . . . exponentially. In winter, a good solution is to turn on the oven to "warm." Place the dough loaf (ready to bake) in the oven, covering it with a heavy mist of water. Turn off the oven. It should rise in an oven at 100 degrees or less. Once the loaf has risen, pull it out of the oven. Preheat the oven to 375°F and then proceed to bake.*

- LOAF FORMATION: *The loaf-molding technique (p. 67) is a factor in how well the loaf will rise because it is optimal for trapping the air produced by the yeast. The more air that is trapped inside the loaf, the lighter the final loaf will be. See the section in this book on loaf molding for details.*

- FRESHNESS OF THE YEAST AND TYPE OF YEAST: *Checking the freshness of the yeast is always a good idea. If you are using the regular active dry yeast, ½ teaspoon is the correct measurement, but if the yeast is older, you will need more (up to 1 teaspoon). If there is still a problem (like during the winter months), you may add up to ¼ cup sugar or honey to the recipe to help activate the yeast.*

NO-KNEAD FOUR-INGREDIENT WHEAT BREAD

1 loaf or 12 medium-sized dinner rolls

You will notice only a few changes in this recipe from the recipe for the white no-knead bread (p. 13). There is more moisture in the whole wheat recipe. Whole grain will always need more moisture because it contains the fiber and all the parts of the grain. The additional moisture will give your bread a better texture as well as a better shelf life. Whenever possible, use the higher-protein flour made from hard white or hard red wheat. My personal preference is Kamut flour. Kamut flour is made from a grain known as the durum wheat of the ancient Egyptians. It makes exceptional bread and is always organic and non–genetically modified. I grind my own flour, but you can use some that is pre-ground. If you live in a particularly dry environment, you may need to adjust the water and add the full amount listed in the recipe. The dough should be soft and supple.

4 cups hard wheat flour (mill your own or use Kamut flour)

1½ tsp. salt

¼ tsp. instant yeast (or ½ tsp. active dry yeast)

2–2½ cups water (under 110°F)

DIRECTIONS:

1. Combine ingredients in a 1-gallon food-grade bucket (or a 1-gallon bowl with a lid) until everything is mixed and smooth. Combining everything takes 20–30 turns by hand.

2. Cover with a lid and keep covered at room temperature until you're ready to bake bread, 10–12 hours.

DIRECTIONS CONTINUED ON NEXT PAGE

DIRECTIONS CONTINUED:

BAKING A LOAF:

Form dough into a loaf and place on a lightly oiled baking stone or in a greased 8-inch loaf pan. Allow to rise in a warm room until doubled, about 2 hours. Bake at 375°F for 35–40 minutes (meat thermometer will register 165°F or more). Enjoy!

BAKING DINNER ROLLS:

Divide dough into 12 rolls and form according to the roll-molding tips on page 68. Place on a lightly greased baking sheet, 2 inches apart, and allow to raise until doubled, 2–2½ hours. Lightly mist with water and bake in a preheated 425-degree oven for 20–25 minutes.

CHEF'S NOTE:

See Chef's Notes on page 14 for troubleshooting specifics.

OVERNIGHT HAPPINESS BREAD

2 standard-sized loaves or 24 medium-sized dinner rolls

Overnight bread has remarkable depth of flavor and makes outstandingly delicious loaves. I prefer this longer fermentation with really good whole wheat flour because the taste is unmistakably complex compared to bread made with a quick ferment. This bread is made in two stages, starting with a sponge, or pre-dough, several hours before you actually intend to bake. The yeast in the sponge, when introduced to the newer yeast in the second step, will make for a faster rise. Like anything in life, a slow, long development in the beginning will result in the most sophisticated and beautiful creations. That can certainly be said of this bread. It is elegant and simple, one of a kind, and worth the wait.

SPONGE:

¼ tsp. yeast

1 cup cold water

2 cups whole wheat bread flour

⅓ cup instant potato flakes

½ tsp. salt

SPONGE DIRECTIONS:

1. Combine all ingredients in an 8-cup mixing bowl (nonmetal works best). Combining will take about 5 minutes. Cover and leave in a cool room until you are ready to bake the bread, 12–18 hours. If you will be leaving it for more than 18 hours, it can be stored in the fridge part of the time, or stir it after 8 hours. This will keep the yeast happy, moving it to greener pastures, and will evaporate any alcohol produced by the fermentation process that would otherwise hurt the yeast's ability to raise the bread. After 12–18 hours, it will be really puffy and smell like a good yeasty bread dough. Remember to keep it rather cool during this overnight period.

DIRECTIONS CONTINUED ON NEXT PAGE

DOUGH INGREDIENTS:

- 2 cups lukewarm water
- 2 Tbsp. honey
- 2 tsp. active dry yeast
- 2 tsp. salt
- 4 cups whole wheat bread flour
- ¼ cup olive oil

DIRECTIONS:

1. Put sponge in mixer and add water, honey, and active dry yeast and mix well until sponge is broken up. Add salt, flour, and olive oil and knead for 5 minutes at medium speed with a dough hook.

2. Form dough into a ball. This makes a balloon-like structure that helps hold in the fermenting gases and helps the texture of the bread.

3. Lightly spray top of dough with water. This keeps it moist, which ensures no lumps of crusty dough in the bread. Cover dough with plastic wrap in a bowl and allow it to rise at room temperature (75–80 degrees) for 1½–2 hours, until doubled in size.

4. Take dough out of bowl. Punch all air out of dough and reform into a ball. Spray bowl and dough ball with water again. Place dough in bowl, cover with plastic, and allow it to rise once more.

BAKING STANDARD LOAVES:

Lightly coat two 8×4 baking pans with oil and dust with cornmeal. Lightly mist a clean countertop with water. Take dough out of bowl and place on countertop. Divide dough in half. Form each loaf using loaf-molding technique on page 67. Lightly coat top of loaves with melted butter and then lightly tent loaves with plastic or plastic bags, or place in a moist place to rise. Allow to rise until dough is ½ inch above edge of pans, 1–1½ hours. Lightly slit tops of loaves with a very sharp knife. Bake in preheated 425-degree oven for 20 minutes and then drop the temperature to 350 for the final 15–20 minutes of baking. Remove from pans and allow to cool completely before cutting.

BAKING DINNER ROLLS:

Divide dough into 24 rolls and form according to roll-molding tips on page 68. Place rolls on a lightly greased baking sheet, 2 inches apart, and allow to rise until doubled, 1–1½ hours. Lightly mist with water and bake in a preheated 425-degree oven for 20–25 minutes.

MOM'S FIVE-DAY BREAD

4 standard-sized loaves or 48 medium-sized rolls

My mother, Geneve, developed this bread dough recipe a bazillion years ago in a galaxy far, far away . . . or so it seems. Life has taken me far from my mother's home, but her recipe for this remarkable bread will always be a classic. It is called five-day bread, but the dough can be made up to seven days ahead of time. The dough is stored in a large bucket or covered bowl in the fridge. I love this dough! It can be made into rolls, pretzels, pizzas, and, yes, decorative bread loaves. This dough is excellent to keep on hand for all your breadmaking needs. Don't be dismayed by the number of ingredients in this recipe—each one works with the other to make it perfect.

2 Tbsp. active dry yeast

4 cups milk (cold is best)

¾ cup honey

4 eggs

¾ cup oil

1½ cups mashed potatoes, cooled to body temperature

1 Tbsp. baking powder

2 cups whole wheat bread flour

12–14 cups bread flour

1 Tbsp. salt

DIRECTIONS:

1. Dissolve yeast in milk. Stir in honey. Allow yeast to get foamy.
2. Add eggs, oil, mashed potatoes, baking powder, whole wheat flour, 2 cups bread flour, and salt, in that order. Beat until smooth.
3. Allow dough to rest for 10–15 minutes.
4. Add enough of the remaining flour to make soft dough that is easy to handle but not dry. Turn dough onto a lightly floured surface and knead for 10 minutes (about 600 turns). You can also use an electric stand-mixer on medium speed, 5–6 minutes. Form dough into a ball

DIRECTIONS CONTINUED ON NEXT PAGE

DIRECTIONS CONTINUED:

and place in an ungreased 2-gallon bowl or food-grade bucket with lid. (If you don't have a large enough bowl, use 2 smaller bowls, or half the recipe if you are worried about the dough growing outside its container all over your fridge.) Put container in fridge, tightly covered. Punch dough down after 2 hours, or earlier if you use warm ingredients or flour. If dough is over 85 degrees when you put it in fridge, be sure to punch down sooner.

5. Form dough into a ball again.
6. Cover tightly and chill for at least 8 hours. Punch dough down daily if keeping it more than a day or two (this not only expels gas but also ensures even temperature in the dough).
7. You can use this dough in any of the white bread, roll, or marble-loaf applications.

BAKING STANDARD LOAVES:

Divide dough into 4 equal portions. Form each loaf using loaf-molding technique on page 67. Lightly coat tops of loaves with melted butter and then lightly tent loaves with plastic or plastic bags, or place in a moist place to rise. Allow to rise until dough is ½ inch above the edge of the pan, 1–1½ hours. Lightly slit tops of loaves with a very sharp knife. Bake in preheated 425-degree oven for 20 minutes and then drop the temperature to 350 for the final 15–20 minutes of baking. Remove from pans and allow to cool completely before cutting.

BAKING DINNER ROLLS:

Divide dough into 48 rolls and form according to roll-molding tips on page 68. Place rolls on a lightly greased baking sheet, 2 inches apart, and allow to rise until doubled, 1–1½ hours. Lightly mist with water and bake in a preheated 425-degree oven for 20–25 minutes.

BASIC SWEET BREAD

2 standard-sized loaves or 24 medium-sized dinner rolls

2 cups water (no hotter than 110 degrees)

2 tsp. (1 packet) SAF instant yeast, rapid rise

½ cup sugar

6½–7 cups bread flour

1 Tbsp. salt

½ cup oil

2 large eggs

Delicious, lightly sweet bread is always great to have around. This is our family favorite. Made with the addition of a little oil and egg, it will have a longer shelf life than bread that is made with only flour and water. This recipe also uses rapid-rise (SAF) yeast, and it calls for a method of mixing known by bakers as the straight dough method. *All the ingredients are mixed together in one bowl at one time. There's no fuss and there's certainly no frustration. It is a great bread dough to make for quick dinner rolls or a last-minute gathering.*

DIRECTIONS:

1. Combine all ingredients in a large bowl or mixer.
2. Knead for 5 minutes by hand or 3 minutes in a mixer on medium setting.
3. Form dough into a ball and place in an ungreased bowl covered with plastic or a lid for 1 hour, or until doubled in size.
4. Punch dough down. You can form this dough into any of the sweet bread recipe loaves as specified per recipe.

BAKING STANDARD LOAVES:

Divide dough in half. Form each loaf using the loaf-molding technique on page 67. Lightly coat tops of loaves with melted butter, and then lightly tent loaves with plastic or plastic bags, or place

in a moist place to rise. Allow to rise until dough is ½ inch above the edge of the pan, 1–1½ hours. Lightly slit tops of loaves with a very sharp knife. Bake in preheated 425-degree oven for 20 minutes and then drop the temperature to 350 for the final 15–20 minutes of baking. Remove from pans and allow to cool completely before cutting.

BAKING DINNER ROLLS:

Divide dough into 24 rolls and form according to the roll-molding tips on page 68. Place rolls on a lightly greased baking sheet, 2 inches apart, and allow to rise until doubled, 1–1½ hours. Lightly mist with water and bake in a preheated 425-degree oven for 20–25 minutes.

BASIC WHITE BREAD

2 standard-sized loaves or 24 medium-sized dinner rolls

This good all-purpose bread dough lends itself well to the addition of savory herbs, seeds, nuts, and spices. Keep the dough soft and knead it well. You'll find this one to be a perfect base for any of the decorative loaves in this book.

2 cups water (no hotter than 110 degrees)

2 tsp. (1 packet) yeast, rapid rise

1 Tbsp. sugar

6 cups unbleached bread flour

1½ tsp. salt

6 Tbsp. oil

DIRECTIONS:

1. Combine everything in a large bowl or mixer (this is the straight dough mixing method).
2. Knead for 5 minutes by hand or 3 minutes in a mixer on medium setting.
3. Form dough into a ball and place in an ungreased bowl covered with plastic or a lid for 1 hour, or until doubled in size.
4. Punch dough down. You can form this bread into any of the white bread technique loaves as specified per recipe.

BAKING STANDARD LOAVES:

For standard loaves, divide dough in half. Form each loaf using the loaf-molding technique on page 67. Lightly coat tops of loaves with melted butter, and then lightly tent loaves with plastic or plastic bags, or place in a moist place to rise. Allow to rise until dough is ½ inch above the edge of the pan, 1–1½ hours. Lightly slit tops of loaves with a very sharp knife. Bake in preheated 425-degree oven for 20 minutes and then drop the temperature to 350 for the final 15–20 minutes of baking. Remove from pans and allow to cool completely before cutting.

BAKING DINNER ROLLS:

Divide dough into 24 rolls and form according to the roll-molding tips on page 68. Place rolls on a lightly greased baking sheet, 2 inches apart, and allow to rise until doubled, 1–1½ hours. Lightly mist with water and bake in a preheated 425-degree oven for 20–25 minutes.

BASIC WHOLE WHEAT BREAD

2 standard-sized loaves or 24 medium-sized dinner rolls

This is a staple recipe for any whole grain, 100 percent wheat sandwich or decorative loaf. The flavor is really outstanding. Because the recipe is lower in sweetener, it lends itself well to the addition of savory herbs and spices as well as cheeses and spicy peppers. The directions are in place to make sandwich loaves with it, but really, any of the decorative loaves can be made using this base.

Chef's Note: *Use the dough from this recipe in any of the techniques that call for basic wheat bread for baking.*

2 tsp. active dry yeast

½ cup cool water

6 cups whole wheat bread flour

2 tsp. salt

2½ cups lukewarm water

2 Tbsp. honey

¼ cup oil

DIRECTIONS:

1. Dissolve yeast in ½ cup cool water. Mix flour and salt in a large bowl and make a well in the mixture.
2. Dissolve honey in the 2½ cups water and add oil. Pour this liquid and yeast mixture into well of flour. Stirring from the center, first combine ingredients to make a smooth batter. Then fold in the remaining flour from sides of bowl, mixing them together into a soft dough.
3. Wait 10 minutes—then evaluate dough. Dough should be supple and not overly dry.
4. Add more water or flour if required and knead dough about 600 strokes without adding any more flour. (This takes about 6 minutes on medium speed in a KitchenAid mixer.) Dough should remain soft and should become elastic and smooth.
5. Form dough into a ball and put in an ungreased crock. Cover tightly with plastic wrap or a lid and allow fermenting—at about 80 degrees, this will take 1½–2 hours.

DIRECTIONS CONTINUED ON PAGE 30

DIRECTIONS CONTINUED:

6. Wet your finger and poke it into dough. If your finger goes in without much resistance and the hole remains when your finger is removed, the dough is ready to be punched down. Punch dough down. For best results, do not wait until it sighs and collapses when poked.

7. Gently press out accumulated gas: turn the dough out onto a lightly floured table and, keeping the smooth surface carefully unbroken, deflate the dough by pressing it with your wet or floury hand from one side to another.

BAKING STANDARD LOAVES:

Divide dough in half. Form each loaf using the loaf-molding technique on page 67. Lightly coat tops of loaves with melted butter, and then lightly tent loaves with plastic or plastic bags, or place in a moist place to rise. Allow to rise until dough is ½ inch above the edge of the pan, 1–1½ hours. Lightly slit tops of loaves with a very sharp knife. Bake in preheated 425-degree oven for 20 minutes and then drop the temperature to 350 for the final 15–20 minutes of baking. Remove from pans and allow to cool completely before cutting.

BAKING DINNER ROLLS:

Divide dough into 24 rolls and form according to the roll-molding tips on page 68. Place rolls on a lightly greased baking sheet, 2 inches apart, and allow to rise until doubled, 1–1½ hours. Lightly mist with water and bake in a preheated 425-degree oven for 20–25 minutes.

IRISH SODA BREAD

1 round loaf or 16 rolls

Irish soda bread is a quick bread made with baking soda. Be sure to get all the clumps out of your baking soda by rubbing it through a fine mesh strainer or between your fingers. Biting into a clump of baking soda is probably the last thing you want to do when tasting bread. This is the only bread recipe in this book where I actually recommend the use of lower-protein flour, like cake flour, for the base. It is a totally different bread than breads I make with yeast, but it is outstanding.

4 cups cake flour (if you use all-purpose, be especially careful not to overmix)

1 Tbsp. baking soda

½ cup sugar

¼ tsp. salt

¼ cup butter

1 cup dark raisins

1 Tbsp. caraway seeds (optional)

1 cup cold milk

DIRECTIONS:

1. Preheat oven to 400°F.
2. Prepare a baking sheet by spraying it lightly with cooking spray or lining it with parchment paper.
3. Sift flour, baking soda, sugar, and salt together into a large bowl. Using a pastry cutter or 2 knives, cut butter into the dry ingredients until it resembles coarse meal.
4. Add raisins, caraway seeds (if desired), and milk. Mix dough until just combined; avoid overmixing, which will cause the dough to toughen.
5. Turn dough onto a lightly floured surface. Press dough into a ball (I roll it in oats). Form dough into a round loaf, or cut into 16 equal pieces to make rolls. Dust with flour and lightly score an *X* across the top of each roll or loaf with a sharp knife.

DIRECTIONS CONTINUED ON NEXT PAGE

DIRECTIONS CONTINUED:

6. Bake the soda bread at over 165°F until it is lightly browned, 35–40 minutes for a loaf, 8–10 minutes for rolls.

7. Wrap the bread in a tea towel directly out of the oven. Cool the soda bread in the tea towel on a wire rack before serving. It can be held at room temperature for up to 2 days or frozen for up to 4 weeks. I like it best right out of the oven!

OAT BREAD

2 standard-sized loaves or 24 medium-sized dinner rolls

The addition of a rolled oat or grain to a bread recipe, if done incorrectly, can lead to a very dense, overly dry loaf. We call these loaves "paperweights made in the oven." But this is not the case with this oat bread recipe. The secret lies in soaking the oats at the beginning, as outlined in the directions. This method hydrates the oats, making them pliable and moist, which will make your bread tender and delicious!

3 cups old-fashioned rolled oats

2½ cups water or milk (no hotter than 110 degrees)

½ cup honey

¼ cup olive oil

2 tsp. active dry yeast

3 cups whole wheat bread flour

1 Tbsp. salt

DIRECTIONS:

1. In a large bowl, combine oats, water or milk, honey, olive oil, and yeast. Allow oats to absorb water and the yeast to get active, about 30 minutes.

2. Add whole wheat bread flour and salt to bowl. You may need more or less flour depending on flour's storing conditions. I usually opt for less flour whenever possible. More makes pretty stiff dough.

3. Knead dough by hand in bowl for 300 turns, and avoid using too much flour in kneading. Or you can use a mixer, which will take 3–4 minutes on medium speed. Form dough into a ball and place in an ungreased, covered, gallon-sized bowl. Allow to rise until doubled.

DIRECTIONS CONTINUED ON NEXT PAGE

DIRECTIONS CONTINUED:

BAKING STANDARD LOAVES:

Divide dough in half. Form each loaf using the loaf-molding technique on page 67. Lightly coat tops of loaves with melted butter, and then lightly tent loaves with plastic or plastic bags, or place in a moist place to rise. Allow to rise until dough is ½ inch above the edge of the pan, 1–1½ hours. Lightly slit tops of loaves with a very sharp knife. Bake in preheated 425-degree oven for 20 minutes and then drop the temperature to 350 for the final 15–20 minutes of baking. Remove from pans and allow to cool completely before cutting.

BAKING DINNER ROLLS:

Divide dough into 24 rolls and form according to the roll-molding tips on page 68. Place rolls on a lightly greased baking sheet, 2 inches apart, and allow to rise until doubled, 1–1½ hours. Lightly mist with water and bake in a preheated 425-degree oven for 20–25 minutes.

DOUBLE CHOCOLATE BREAD

2 standard-sized loaves or baguettes, or 24 medium-sized dessert/breakfast rolls

When it comes to a good brown bread, I adore rye bread. However, I'm an ever bigger fan of chocolate. Here's a fun yeast-raised chocolate loaf that is sure to please. I'm also particularly fond of the addition of fresh orange zest or anise seed. To me, this bread is better than a piece of cake and a whole lot easier to make and decorate! Try using this bread the next time you make French toast for breakfast. You'll never want to go back to plain white bread. I often marble the chocolate dough with white sweet dough for a totally different take on a standard marbled loaf.

½ cup unsalted butter

4 (1-oz.) squares unsweetened baker's chocolate

1 Tbsp. (1 packet) active dry yeast

1½ cups lukewarm water (no hotter than 110 degrees)

½ cup brown sugar

5½–6 cups bread flour, divided

2 tsp. salt

1 Tbsp. double-strength vanilla

2 large eggs

8 oz. high-quality chocolate chips (if making baguettes)

1 egg white (if making baguettes)

2 Tbsp. water (if making baguettes)

DIRECTIONS:

1. Combine and melt butter and unsweetened chocolate slowly over a double boiler or in the microwave at 15-second intervals. Stir often as to not burn the chocolate.
2. In a large bowl, combine yeast, lukewarm water, brown sugar, and about 1 cup flour. When chocolate mixture is completely melted, allow to cool so that it doesn't feel warm to the touch. Mix into flour and yeast mixture. Add salt, vanilla, eggs, and remaining flour except about ½ cup.
3. Knead by hand for 5–7 minutes until soft, supple dough is formed. Very little if any of the remaining flour is needed to keep this dough from sticking to the work surface if you have followed the recipe correctly.

DIRECTIONS CONTINUED ON NEXT PAGE

4. Place dough in a 2-gallon covered bowl and allow to rise for about 2 hours, until doubled in size.

5. Punch dough down. You can use this dough in any of the decorative loaf applications where you want a dark loaf of sweet bread.

BAKING STANDARD LOAVES:

Divide dough in half. Form each loaf using the loaf-molding technique on page 67. Lightly coat tops of loaves with melted butter, and then lightly tent loaves with plastic or plastic bags, or place in a moist place to rise. Allow to rise until dough is ½ inch above the edge of the pan, 1–1½ hours. Lightly slit tops of loaves with a very sharp knife. Bake in preheated 425-degree oven for 20 minutes and then drop the temperature to 350 for the final 15–20 minutes of baking. Remove from pans and allow to cool completely before cutting.

BAKING DINNER ROLLS:

Divide dough into 24 rolls and form according to the roll-molding tips on page 68. Place rolls on a lightly greased baking sheet, 2 inches apart, and allow to rise until doubled, 1–1½ hours. Lightly mist with water and bake in a preheated 425-degree oven for 20–25 minutes.

BAKING BAGUETTES:

Divide dough in half. Roll out into a 14×10 rectangle and spread half the chocolate chips onto each dough half, leaving an inch around the outside edges. It helps to lightly roll a rolling pin over the chocolate chips to ease them into dough. Be careful not to push them through—just nestle them in. Tightly roll dough into long logs, encasing the chocolate chips. Don't make them longer than your sheet pans. When they are rolled, place loaves seam side down on a lightly oiled sheet pan or pan lined with parchment paper. Cover each loaf lightly with plastic wrap or place in an unheated oven, lightly spraying it with a mist of water. Let rise for 1½–2 hours, until very fluffy. Remove wrapping or take out of cool oven. Preheat oven to 375°F. Take 1 egg white and 2 tablespoons of water and whisk together in a bowl. Using a pastry brush, lightly coat the top of the bread with the egg mixture. Lightly slash with a sharp knife across the top of the bread. Bake for 40–45 minutes or until temperature on a meat thermometer reads over 170°F. When baked, the outside will be smooth and shiny. The inside will be studded with chocolate chips. Well, that is unless a few peek out through the slash marks.

CHEF TESS'S WHOLE GRAIN, CHOCOLATE, HONEY, AMARANTH BREAD

2 standard-sized loaves or baguettes, or 24 medium-sized dessert/breakfast rolls

This 100 percent whole grain chocolate loaf is sure to please. I add some honey and popped amaranth seeds to the bread, giving it the taste and depth of a toasted nut without the added fat. I love it with a hint of cayenne pepper and cinnamon to lend a new level of complexity to the taste.

½ cup orange-infused olive oil

4 (1-oz.) squares unsweetened baker's chocolate

1 Tbsp. (1 packet) active dry yeast

1½ cups lukewarm water (no hotter than 110 degrees)

½ cup honey

5½ cups whole Kamut flour or whole wheat bread flour, divided

¼ cup organic amaranth (1 cup when popped)

2 tsp. salt

1 Tbsp. double-strength vanilla

2 tsp. cayenne pepper

1 Tbsp. Chef Tess Wise Woman of the East spice blend or pumpkin pie spice

2 large eggs

8 oz. high-quality chocolate chips (if making baguettes)

1 egg white (if making baguettes)

2 Tbsp. water (if making baguettes)

DIRECTIONS:

1. Combine the olive oil and baker's unsweetened chocolate and melt slowly over a double boiler or in the microwave for 15-second intervals. Stir often so as to not burn the chocolate.
2. In a large bowl, combine the yeast, warm water, honey, and about 1 cup flour. When the chocolate mixture is completely melted, allow to cool so that it doesn't feel warm to the touch.
3. Pop the amaranth: Heat a large deep pan for 2–3 minutes on high heat. Add the ¼ cup amaranth and stir with a wooden spoon until it pops.
4. Mix the amaranth into the water, flour, and yeast mixture. Add the salt, vanilla, spices, eggs, and remaining flour except about ½ cup.
5. Knead by hand for 5–7 minutes until soft, supple dough is formed. Very little if any of the remaining flour is needed to keep this dough from sticking to the work surface if you have followed the recipe correctly. Place dough in a 2-gallon covered bowl and allow to rise for about 2 hours, until doubled in size. Punch down dough.

BAKING STANDARD LOAVES:

Divide dough in half. Form each loaf using the loaf-molding technique on page 67. Lightly coat tops of loaves with melted butter, and then lightly tent loaves with plastic or plastic bags, or place in a moist place to rise. Allow to rise until dough is ½ inch above the edge of the pan, 1–1½ hours. Lightly slit tops of loaves with a very sharp knife. Bake in preheated 425-degree oven for 20 minutes and then drop the temperature to 350 for the final 15–20 minutes of baking. Remove from pans and allow to cool completely before cutting.

BAKING DINNER ROLLS:

Divide dough into 24 rolls and form according to the roll-molding tips on page 68. Place rolls on a lightly greased baking sheet, 2 inches apart, and allow to rise until doubled, 1–1½ hours. Lightly mist with water and bake in a preheated 425-degree oven for 20–25 minutes.

DIRECTIONS CONTINUED ON NEXT PAGE

DIRECTIONS CONTINUED:

BAKING BAGUETTES:

Divide dough in half. Roll out into a 14×10 rectangle and spread half the chocolate chips onto each dough half, leaving an inch around the outside edges. It helps to lightly roll a rolling pin over the chocolate chips to ease them into dough. Be careful not to push them through—just nestle them in. Tightly roll dough into long logs, encasing the chocolate chips. Don't make them longer than your sheet pans. When they are rolled, place loaves seam side down on a lightly oiled sheet pan or pan lined with parchment paper. Cover each loaf lightly with plastic wrap or place in an unheated oven, lightly spraying it with a mist of water. Let rise for 1½–2 hours, until very fluffy. Remove wrapping or take out of cool oven. Preheat oven to 375°F. Take 1 egg white and 2 tablespoons of water and whisk together in a bowl. Using a pastry brush, lightly coat the top of the bread with the egg mixture. Lightly slash with a sharp knife across the top of the bread. Bake for 40–45 minutes or until temperature on a meat thermometer reads over 170°F. When baked, the outside will be smooth and shiny. The inside will be studded with chocolate chips. Well, that is unless a few peek out through the slash marks.

OLD-FASHIONED PEASANT'S RYE BREAD

2 standard-sized loaves or 24 medium-sized dinner rolls

This nice, mild, 100 percent whole grain rye bread ends up fluffy and delightful. Rye grain is lower in protein, so be sure to use good high-protein wheat flour in conjunction with your rye flour for a good texture in your finished product. Rye flour is, by nature, a grayish-looking flour. The addition of molasses and baker's cocoa are needed to give this bread a good deep color. This rye bread calls for buttermilk, apple balsamic vinegar, and a relative of garlic known as a shallot. The flavor is unique. And if you love a good rye, this bread will become a favorite.

- 2 tsp. active dry yeast
- ¼ cup warm water (max 110 degrees)
- 1¼ cups buttermilk
- ¾ cup water
- 1 Tbsp. caraway seeds, toasted
- ¼ cup unsweetened powdered cocoa
- 2 Tbsp. oil
- 2 Tbsp. apple balsamic vinegar
- 2 Tbsp. molasses
- 5½ cups whole wheat bread flour, divided
- 2½ tsp. salt
- 1 cup 100 percent whole grain rye flour
- 1–2 large shallots, pressed

DIRECTIONS:

1. In a small dish, combine the yeast and warm water. Let it rest until it bubbles, about 5 minutes.

2. In a mixing bowl, combine the buttermilk, ¾ cup water, caraway seeds, cocoa, oil, and apple balsamic vinegar.

3. Add the yeast/water combination to the bowl. Add the molasses. Add 5 cups whole wheat bread flour and the salt. Knead dough in your mixer on medium-low speed for 5 minutes. Turn off mixer and add the rye flour and pressed shallots. Continue to knead the dough on medium-low speed for 5 more minutes. Turn off the mixer and allow the dough to sit for 10 minutes.

4. After the dough rests, mix for 2-3 more minutes, adding just enough flour for the dough to really climb up the dough hook. Turn off the machine and dump the dough onto a light water–misted countertop and form dough into a ball. Clean out the mixing bowl and return the dough to the bowl. Cover with plastic and allow to rise for 1½–2 hours.

5. Expel excess gas by pressing down on the dough. Form the dough into a ball again, and cover with plastic for a second rise, 45–60 minutes. You can use this dough in any decorative bread recipe that calls for dark dough.

BAKING STANDARD LOAVES:

From the dough into 2 sandwich loaves, using the loaf-molding tips on page 67, in two 8×4 greased bread pans. When formed, lightly mist with water and allow to rise for 45–60 minutes. Mist with water again and sprinkle with caraway seeds or apply decorative dough. Preheat oven to 425°F the last few minutes of rising. Bake for 15 minutes and then lower oven temperature to 350 and bake for 20–25 more minutes until it reaches an internal temperature of 175°F.

BAKING DINNER ROLLS:

Divide dough into 24 rolls and form according to the roll-molding tips on page 68. Place rolls on a lightly greased baking sheet, 2 inches apart, and allow to rise until doubled, 1–1½ hours. Lightly mist with water and bake in a preheated 425-degree oven for 20–25 minutes.

YEAST-RAISED ORANGE GINGERBREAD

2 standard-sized loaves or 24 medium-sized breakfast rolls

I developed this yeast-raised gingerbread recipe several years ago when I wanted to make decorative Christmas bread wreathes. A star was born with a sprinkle of minced candied ginger and all the spice and magic of the holiday season. I absolutely adore this bread when it is served toasted with a slather of honey butter right next to a big mug of homemade eggnog. It makes a wonderful addition to any festive buffet or Christmas wedding. For an extra amazing cinnamon roll, use this dough instead of your regular white dough.

½ cup dark molasses

2 cups water (75–80 degrees)

½ cup melted butter

1 Tbsp. active dry yeast

½ cup sugar

1 tsp. rum extract

1 tsp. brandy extract

6 cups high-gluten bread flour

¼ cup minced candied ginger

1 Tbsp. anise seed

zest of 1 orange

1 tsp. salt

1 Tbsp. Chef Tess Wise Woman of the East spice blend or 2 tsp. cinnamon

1 Tbsp. baking powder

DIRECTIONS:

1. Combine molasses, water, melted butter, yeast, sugar, and extracts in a medium bowl. In a bread mixer, combine the flour, ginger, anise seed, orange zest, salt, spice blend, and baking powder.

2. Add the liquid mixture to the bread mixer and lightly combine by hand until moistened. Attach dough hook. On low speed, mix the dough for 4–5 minutes until elastic and smooth.

3. Remove hook and form the dough into a ball. Place in a covered bowl in a warm place and allow to rise (at 80 degrees it takes about 1½ hours).

4. Expel the air from the dough. You can use this dough in any recipe where a dark dough is needed (this dough is great for cinnamon rolls as well).

BAKING STANDARD LOAVES:

Divide dough in half. Form each loaf using the loaf-molding technique on page 67. Lightly coat tops of loaves with melted butter, and then lightly tent loaves with plastic or plastic bags, or place in a moist place to rise. Allow to rise until dough is ½ inch above the edge of the pan, 1–1½ hours. Lightly slit tops of loaves with a very sharp knife. Bake in preheated 425-degree oven for 20 minutes and then drop the temperature to 350 for the final 15–20 minutes of baking. Remove from pans and allow to cool completely before cutting.

BAKING DINNER ROLLS:

Divide dough into 24 rolls and form according to the roll-molding tips on page 68. Place rolls on a lightly greased baking sheet, 2 inches apart, and allow to rise until doubled, 1–1½ hours. Lightly mist with water and bake in a preheated 425-degree oven for 20–25 minutes.

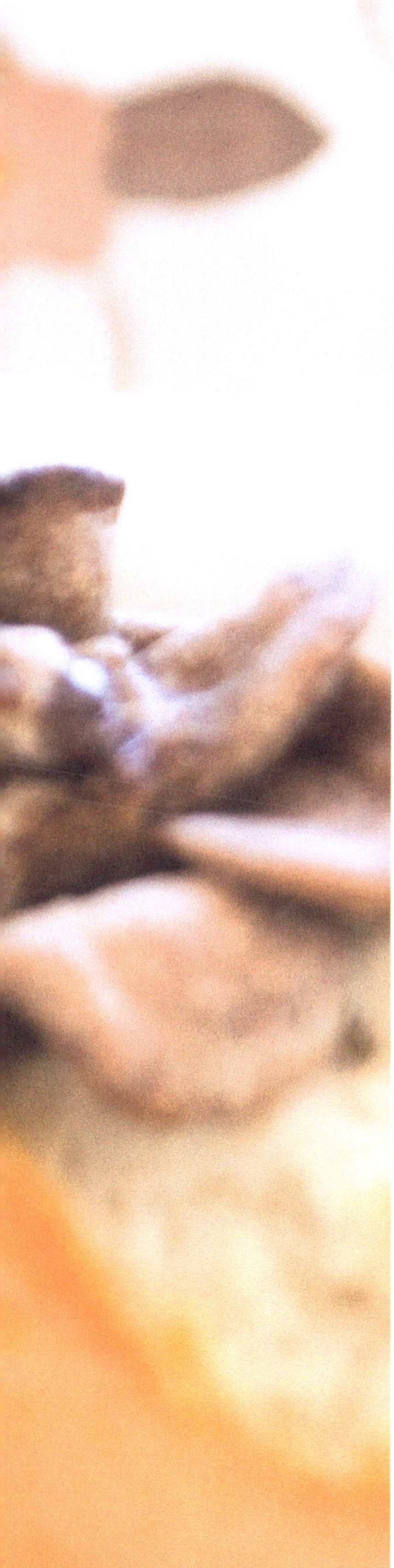

SIMPLE DECORATIVE DOUGH EMBELLISHMENTS

There is a method to my madness when it comes to adding embellishment dough on bread loaves. I have seen many loaves of decorated breads that have been covered in shellac, to be used as pure decoration at bakeries or in homes. Many of these are pretty but are obviously not intended to be eaten. I completely expect you to make bread and eat it. Even the most beautiful of my loaves is designed to be consumed in culinary bliss. Thus the addition and development of edible decorative dough has come to pass.

You can use cutting tools for ornate decorative bread dough, and many cake decorating and cookie cutter companies make leaf and flower cutting tools.

SIMPLE DECORATIVE DOUGH EMBELLISHMENT TUTORIAL

All of the recipes in this section use the following dough embellishment technique:

1. Combine all ingredients and knead until pliable dough is formed.
2. Lightly flour a tabletop. Keep dough that is not being worked in a covered container. Roll a ball of dough flat, to 1/16-inch thickness, keeping the surface of the table lightly floured.
3. Cut out desired shapes.
4. Allow your loaf of bread to rise and bake according to recipe directions. About 15 minutes before the loaf is completely baked (as it reaches an internal temperature of 165°F), remove from the oven.
5. Mist the top of the loaf with a heavy coat of water. Carefully arrange embellishments on the top of the loaf according to your preference.
6. Return the loaf to the hot oven on the center rack and allow to cook for 15–20 more minutes, until the loaf is golden brown and the embellishments are crispy.

SAVORY HERB DECORATIVE DOUGH

I use several edible decorative dough recipes, but this savory version I reserve for the tasty herb, hot pepper, or cheese breads. It is similar in taste to a crispy cracker when baked on top of the loaf.

1 cup oat flour

1 cup all-purpose flour

2 tsp. salt

2 Tbsp. sugar

½ cup + 2 Tbsp. water (colored if you want the dough to have a tint)

½ tsp. onion powder

½ tsp. garlic powder

1 Tbsp. finely minced fresh herbs

DIRECTIONS:

1. Combine all the ingredients and knead until pliable dough is formed.
2. Lightly flour a tabletop. Keep dough that is not being worked in a covered container. Roll a ball of dough flat, to 1/16-inch thickness, keeping the surface of the table lightly floured.
3. Cut out desired shapes.
4. Allow your loaf of bread to rise, and bake according to recipe directions. About 15 minutes before the loaf is completely baked (as it reaches an internal temperature of 165°F), remove from the oven.
5. Mist the top of the loaf with a heavy coat of water. Carefully arrange embellishments on the top of the loaf according to your preference.
6. Return the loaf to the hot oven on the center rack and allow to cook for 15–20 more minutes, until the loaf is golden brown and the embellishments are crispy.
7. Decorate the loaf with the painted bread technique or glitter or pearl as desired.

SWEET SPICED DECORATIVE DOUGH

Use this slightly sweet, spiced decorative dough on all your sweet breads. It will give you beautiful, lightly caramelized dough on top of the loaves and a naturally beautiful look to any embellishment.

1 cup oat flour

1 cup all-purpose flour

2 tsp. salt

⅓ cup sugar

½ cup + 2 Tbsp. water (colored if you want the dough to have a tint)

1 tsp. cinnamon

½ tsp. ground cardamom

DIRECTIONS:

1. Combine all the ingredients and knead until pliable dough is formed.
2. Lightly flour a tabletop. Keep dough that is not being worked in a covered container. Roll a ball of dough flat, to 1⁄16-inch thickness, keeping the surface of the table lightly floured.
3. Cut out desired shapes.
4. Bake your sweet dough loaf according to recipe directions. About 15 minutes before the loaf is completely baked (as it reaches an internal temperature of 165°F), remove from the oven.
5. Heavily mist the top of your bread with water and carefully arrange the dough embellishments on the loaf. Return the loaf to the oven and bake for about 15 more minutes, until dough is crispy and set.
6. Decorate the loaf with the painted bread technique or glitter or pearl as desired.

OAT DECORATIVE DOUGH

This is the perfect medium-flavored dough to use in either sweet bread or savory bread decorating. I keep a batch of this dough in my fridge up to a week for quick bread fixing.

1 cup oat flour

1 cup all-purpose flour

2 tsp. salt

2 Tbsp. sugar

½ cup + 2 Tbsp. water (colored if you want the dough to have a tint)

½ tsp. onion powder

½ tsp. garlic powder

1 Tbsp. finely minced fresh herbs

DIRECTIONS:

1. Combine all the ingredients and knead until pliable dough is formed.
2. Lightly flour a tabletop. Keep dough that is not being worked in a covered container. Roll a ball of dough flat, to 1/16-inch thickness, keeping the surface of the table lightly floured.
3. Cut out desired shapes.
4. Bake your loaf according to recipe directions. About 15 minutes before the loaf is completely baked (as it reaches an internal temperature of 165°F), remove from the oven.
5. Heavily mist the top of your bread with water and carefully arrange the dough embellishments on the loaf. Return the loaf to the oven and bake for about 15 more minutes, until dough is crispy and set.
6. Decorate the loaf with the painted bread technique or glitter or pearl as desired.

RYE DECORATIVE DOUGH

Sometimes I like to do a darker vine or embellishment on a loaf, and this has been the perfect dough for those special touches. Keep it covered when you're not working it so it doesn't dry out.

1 cup rye flour

1 cup all-purpose flour

2 tsp. salt

¼ cup sugar

2 Tbsp. molasses

½ cup water

1 tsp. ground caraway seed

1 tsp. garlic powder

DIRECTIONS:

1. Combine all the ingredients and knead until pliable dough is formed.
2. Lightly flour a tabletop. Keep dough that is not being worked in a covered container. Roll a ball of dough flat, to 1/16-inch thickness, keeping the surface of the table lightly floured.
3. Cut out desired shapes.
4. Bake your loaf according to recipe directions. About 15 minutes before the loaf is completely baked (as it reaches an internal temperature of 165°F), remove from the oven.
5. Heavily mist the top of your bread with water and carefully arrange the dough embellishments on the loaf. Return the loaf to the oven and bake for about 15 more minutes, until dough is crispy and set.
6. Decorate the loaf with the painted bread technique or added glitter or pearl as desired.

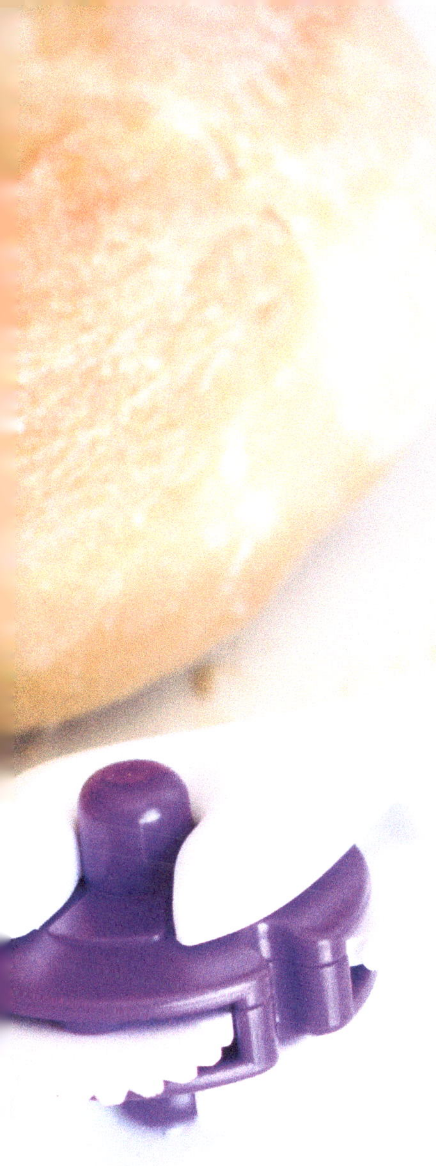

TECHNIQUES OF DECORATIVE LOAF FORMATION

MARBLE LOAF

The first time I ever made a marble rye loaf of bread, I thought to myself, "Why is this method only used for rye bread?" It shouldn't be! I use it to marble any dark and light dough combination. When I do the dough, I make the dark and light dough out of two different recipes in the simple bread recipes section (p. 11). Pick the sweet dough (p. 24) and any of the chocolate doughs or the yeast-raised gingerbread (p. 46) for a sweet loaf. For a savory loaf, any of the white bread, wheat bread, or rye bread recipes will work as your dough base. If you use the full amount of dough as specified for most of the base dough recipes, this method will yield four loaves of bread.

TECHNIQUE:

1. Make 2 different types of dough at the same time so they rise at the same rate. For 2 loaves, you will have 2 pieces of light dough and 2 pieces of dark dough. I suggest Basic White Bread (p. 27) and the dark rye bread (p. 44). Each piece of dough should weigh 8 ounces. The finished loaf should weigh approximately 1 pound. I recommend the use of a kitchen scale to weigh each piece of dough. Make sure you use an equal weight of each kind of dough to make your loaves the same size. This will ease the baking processes.

2. Lightly flour your work surface. Form each piece of dough into a rectangle, about 1 foot by 8 inches.

3. Pat the pieces of dough on a lightly floured surface until they are about the same length and width. Place one dough color on top of the opposite dough color. Press together firmly. Then fold into thirds. Form dough into a log. Place the dough log seam side down onto a lightly oiled sheet pan or into a greased 9×5 loaf pan.

4. Allow dough to rise until doubled in size, 1–1½ hours. Cover the loaf with a very fine mist of oil. This will keep the surface from getting too dry. If you intend to decorate the loaf with embellishments, use a light hand when applying oil (if you use too much oil, the dough embellishments will not stick to loaf correctly).

TECHNIQUE CONTINUED ON NEXT PAGE

TECHNIQUE CONTINUED:

5. Preheat oven to 375°F. Mist the tops of the loaf with water and slash lightly with a very sharp serrated knife, no deeper than ¼ inch into the surface. Cut several 3-inch slits across the top of the loaf (about 2 inches apart). The opposite-colored dough inside the loaf will peek through the holes, creating a decorative effect when baked.

6. Bake for 35–45 minutes, until loaf reaches an internal temperature of 165°F or higher. The bread is now baked through and can be eaten or used for decorative loaves.

7. To embellish loaf, see the simple decorative dough embellishment tutorial on page 50.

LOAF-MOLDING TIPS

The basics on how to fold and mold the structure on a perfect loaf of bread is something that I learned when I first attended a pastry class in culinary school, and it is something I use almost every single day. Master this technique and your bread will suddenly be well-rounded and hold its structure when baked, and you'll find consistency in the overall quality of your bread.

TIPS FOR SUCCESS

- Use very little flour on your work surface when forming loaves. For whole grain bread, I generally use a light mist of water on the surface instead of flour because this tends to make the bread more moist and supple when baked.
- I don't recommend using oil on your hands or work surfaces. Oil acts to shorten gluten strands, but it will also stop bread dough from connecting to its internal structures correctly. If you have ever sliced into a loaf of bread and found that there was a spiral in your loaf (and it wasn't a cinnamon swirl bread), then you may have already experienced this phenomenon.
- Clean your work surfaces between loaves, especially when switching between savory and sweet loaves. This will prevent unwanted savory flavors from showing up in your sweet breads and vice versa.
- Work quickly, using a light hand, but don't be afraid to really press the dough together tightly.
- When adding large chopped nuts, chocolate, and bulky fruits, press them into the dough inside the loaf. This will prevent any burning or off-flavors from occurring when the ingredients are baked.

INSTRUCTIONS FOR MOLDING A STANDARD-SIZED LOAF

A standard-sized loaf of sandwich bread should weigh one pound before baking. I recommend using a kitchen scale when portioning loaves so they will bake evenly and at the same rate. This will affect the final product when baking is done.

1. Lightly flour your work surface and press the dough out into a rectangle approximately 16 inches long and 12 inches wide.
2. Fold the dough into thirds, like a travel brochure.
3. Roll the folded dough into a log and pinch the seams closed as well as the ends of the loaf.
4. Place the loaf seam side down into a lightly greased 8-inch loaf pan. Allow the loaf to rise until doubled in size, making sure the surface of the loaf is covered with a light mist of oil and then tented with a layer of plastic wrap.
5. When the loaf is raised about ½ inch over the edge of the pan, place in a preheated oven and bake according to recipe directions. If you are at a high altitude (over 3,000 feet), you will need to heat your oven to approximately 425°F for the first 15 minutes in order for the loaf to rise correctly and to set the structure of the loaf.

ROLL-MOLDING TIPS

In the simple bread recipes section (p. 11), I have included with the standard yield of bread per recipe the standard yield of dinner rolls, should you decide to use it as roll dough. Here are several tips to successfully produce beautiful rolls.

TIPS FOR SUCCESS

- Divide the dough evenly so the rolls will rise and bake in a uniform amount of time. If there is a big difference in the size of each roll, the small rolls will end up dry and inedible while the large rolls might not cook through.
- Never over-flour work surfaces. Rolling the dough in extra flour will cause undesirable irregular-shaped rolls.
- Roll each piece of dough into a tight round ball, keeping the outer surface rather smooth.
- Pinch the bottom of the roll and place face down. This will trap in as much air as possible and give you fluffier rolls.
- Slightly over-raise the rolls. Unlike sandwich bread, most dinner rolls are best with a very light texture.

DECORATIVE BREAD SLASHING

Decoratively cutting the top of any loaf of bread before it goes in the oven is actually done to help the loaf rise evenly in the hot oven. The cuts help regulate how the steam is expelled from the loaf and will add to the overall shape of your breads.

SLASHING TIPS:

1. Always allow the loaf to rise fully before cutting because cutting will affect the shape of the bread.
2. Preheat the oven fully before cutting the slashes.
3. Use a very sharp or serrated knife and only cut about ¼ inch deep into the surface. Deep slash marks are sometimes desirable but will generally cause the loaf to fall haphazardly in many directions.
4. Small gashes made with sharp kitchen shears will bake and rise to appear like leaves on the surface of your loaf.
5. Applying an egg wash to the loaf before slashing will accentuate the difference in color—the loaf will brown while the dough coming through the open cut will remain light.

BRAIDED BREAD

FOUR-STRAND LOAF

Even though the title of this loaf suggests that there are four strands to be connected, there are in fact only two longer strands that overlap and are then intertwined. Following the picture tutorial will ease your understanding of this process.

TECHNIQUE:

1. Make dough for 1 loaf of bread from any of the simple bread recipes (p. 11).
2. Divide the dough into 2 equal sections and roll the sections into thin strands of equal length, about 1 foot long.
3. Place the strands over one another in a cross.
4. Braid the strands by continually crossing them in opposite directions (see photos).
5. Fold the top strand down and the bottom strand upward.
6. Fold the left strand to the right and cross the right over the left.
7. Cross the vertical strands again.
8. Continue this process until the loaf is completely braided.
9. Tightly pinch the end of the loaf and place on a greased baking sheet.
10. Allow the loaf to rise at room temperature, uncovered, until doubled in size.
11. Preheat oven to 425°F.
12. Bake for 30–35 minutes, until golden brown.
13. Embellish the bread as desired using the decorative techniques in this book.

SIX-STRAND LOAF

This recipe is similar to the Four-Strand Loaf (p. 74), but the process for this one is a little more complex, so pay careful attention to the instructional photos.

TECHNIQUE:

1. Make dough for 1 loaf of bread from any of the simple bread recipes (p. 11).
2. Divide the dough into equal sections and roll the sections into 6 strands of equal length, about 1 foot long.
3. Pinch the strands together tightly at the very end and gently weave the strands in an overlapping motion, twisting the end together. This will take practice, so be patient with yourself.
4. Braid the strands by continually crossing them in opposite directions (see photos).
5. Fold the top strands down and the bottom strands upward.
6. Fold the left strands to the right and cross the right strands over the left in an alternating pattern.
7. Cross the vertical strands again.
8. Continue this process until the loaf is completely braided.
9. Tightly pinch the end of the loaf and place on a greased baking sheet.
10. Allow the loaf to rise at room temperature, uncovered, until doubled in size.
11. Preheat oven to 425°F.
12. Bake for 30–35 minutes, until golden brown.
13. Embellish the bread as desired using the decorative techniques in this book.

THIRTY-TWO-STRAND STAR LOAF

This loaf is by and far the most advanced braid that I do, and it is always met with adoration. It was the first decorative loaf design that I ever sold for a party, and it continues to be the one most requested. I love to make this loaf and then slice the individual star tips to make six different connecting sandwich subs for dramatic dinner presentations. I have included many photos, so follow the picture instructions for success.

TECHNIQUE:

1. Divide the dough from the Basic White Bread recipe (p. 27) into 9 pieces and roll out into long thin strips.
2. Arrange the strips of dough as seen in the first photo. Braid each three-piece section. Dough will be intertwining and will hold the loaf together.
3. Transfer the star loaf to a baking stone or baking sheet. Allow to rise for about 40 minutes. Do not over-proof.
4. Preheat the oven to 375°F and then bake for 40–45 minutes.

OPTIONAL DECORATIONS:

Prepare 1 recipe of Rye Decorative Dough (p. 58). Form rye dough embellishments. Pieces can be made ahead and air-dried for a day or so. Apply a thick layer of water to the top of the bread and gently push embellishments on the bread. You can also make a thin bread paste using equal parts all-purpose flour and water to help hold the pieces to the loaf while baking. Bake dough embellishments on the bread when you bake it. You can also paint details on your bread after baking, using the bread-painting technique (p. 115). Pink bread paint can be made using beet juice or simply using red food coloring combined with a pearl glaze. Use the basic bread-painting technique to add contrasting colors to the braids if desired.

FANCY ROLLS

KNOTS

Each recipe in the simple bread recipes section, when yielding two standard-sized loaves of bread, will generally yield twenty-four medium rolls or one dozen large rolls.

TECHNIQUE:

1. Make dough from one of the simple bread recipes (p. 11). Divide 1 pound of dough into 12 equal balls.
2. Roll each ball into a strip of dough, approximately 8 inches long.
3. Fold each strip in half sideways onto itself.
4. Wrap each piece into a twisted knot, about 3 inches in diameter.
5. Flatten each knot slightly using the heel of your hand.
6. Place the knots on a lightly greased baking sheet, approximately 3 inches apart.
7. Allow the knots to rise until doubled in size, 45–60 minutes.
8. Preheat oven to 425°F.
9. Bake for 15–20 minutes (until they reach an internal temperature of 165°F). Remove the rolls from the oven and allow to cool.

DOUGH EMBELLISHMENTS:

After you've baked the knots, if desired, top with decorative dough embellishments such as flowers and leaves by misting the buns heavily with water. Affix embellishments by pressing firmly but not excessively. Mist again with water and return rolls to the oven. Bake at 350°F for 10–15 more minutes, until decorative dough is crisp.

FANS

A fan roll is a fabulous way to have an herb or spiced pull-apart-layer-by-layer love bomb. Slather butter between each happy layer of dough. They're delightful, fattening, and perfect for any special occasion.

TECHNIQUE:

1. Make dough from one of the simple bread recipes (p. 11). Roll out 1 pound of dough, as you would a cinnamon roll, about ½ inch thick on a lightly floured work surface. Then cover dough with a light layer of butter and sprinkle with your favorite herb combination. (I use my Chef Tess Big Dill seasoning. It is a delightful combination of garlic, onion, bell pepper, citrus, and dill weed.)
2. Cut the dough into 1½-inch strips—the entire length of the dough—and stack the dough strips.
3. Cut the stack into separate 2-inch-long stacks and place each stack sideways into a greased muffin pan.
4. Let dough rise until doubled in size.
5. Preheat oven to 350°F.
6. Bake dough for 25–30 minutes, until golden brown. This technique yields about a dozen rolls.

TWISTS

Each recipe in the simple bread recipes section, when yielding two standard-sized loaves of bread, will generally yield twenty-four medium rolls or one dozen large rolls.

TECHNIQUE:

1. Make dough from one of the simple bread recipes (p. 11). Divide 1 pound of dough into 12 equal balls.
2. Roll each ball into a strip of dough, approximately 8 inches long.
3. Fold each strip of dough in half into itself and twist lightly.
4. Twirl each strip clockwise into a rose-like roll.
5. Place the twists on a lightly oiled baking sheet, approximately 3 inches apart.
6. Allow twists to rise until doubled in size, 45–60 minutes. Preheat oven to 425°F.
7. Bake for 20–25 minutes (until 165°F internal temperature).
8. Remove the twists from the oven and allow to cool.

DOUGH EMBELLISHMENTS:

After you've baked the twists, if desired, mist the rolls with water and gently press dough embellishments into the top of the surface, being careful not to press through the crust. Mist again heavily with water and return to the oven. Bake twists for an additional 10–15 minutes, until the dough embellishments are crisp and golden.

PINWHEELS & CINNAMON ROLLS TIPS

Cinnamon rolls and pinwheels are classic-shaped rolls.

TIPS FOR SUCCESS

- Each simple bread recipe (p. 11) that yields 2 standard-sized loaves will generally make 24 medium-sized cinnamon rolls or savory pinwheels (depending on the sweet or savory dough base you choose).
- Be creative with your flavor additions, but always try to match sweet dough with a slightly sweet filling and vice versa for savory flavors.
- Roll the dough into a rectangular shape for filling. This will ensure that all your rolls are about the same shape and size, effectively standardizing the baking time for all the rolls involved.
- Apply a thin layer of filling so that there aren't too many issues with the buns sticking to your baking sheet or muffin tin.
- Always leave about 1 inch of unfilled dough along the side of the dough where you intend to pinch the dough together. This will ensure that the seam holds together during baking.
- Roll dough tightly enough that the wheels don't fall apart but not so tightly that they cone when baking. It may take a few times making these rolls to master the tension levels for success.

SAVORY FRENCH HERB & SMOKED PAPRIKA PINWHEELS

One of my favorite ways to make a roll taste remarkable is also a fantastic way to make a basket of dinner rolls look like a bouquet full of blooming orange roses. You'll love the savory herbaceous flavor coupled with the complex addition of smoked paprika. See page 89 for pinwheel tips.

TECHNIQUE:

1. Make enough Basic White Bread dough (p. 27) or Basic Whole Wheat Bread dough (p. 28) for 1 loaf. Roll out 1 pound of dough into a 12×8 rectangle.
2. Spread rectangle with a thin layer of butter to the edges and sprinkle with Chef Tess French Provencal Essential spice blend. (This is a bold, rustic blend of herbs, citrus, garlic, and sea salt. I love it with chicken, but I especially love it in buns.)
3. Roll up the dough and cut into 1-inch pinwheels.
4. Place pinwheels in a greased muffin tin and sprinkle lightly with smoked paprika to taste.
5. Allow pinwheels to rise until doubled in size.
6. Preheat oven to 400°F.
7. Bake for 25–30 minutes, until golden. Serve warm.

BEAR CLAWS O' GLORY

This classic breakfast bun can be filled with a wide variety of flavorful blends. Generally I choose a sweet variation, with hazelnut paste, a kiss of ginger, and a touch of lemon. I've also done them with raspberry jam and a little jalapeño. They're excellent as a blue cheese and black pepper roll. And they're amazing as an orange cardamom roll with a hint of lavender or nutmeg. . . . You name it. You can choose any number of flavors. You're only limited by your giant brain and incredible imagination!

TECHNIQUE:

1. Make dough from one of the simple bread recipes (p. 11). Roll out 1 pound of dough into a 12×8 rectangle.
2. Spread rectangle with the filling of your choice. I recommend ½ cup hazelnut butter and a sprinkle of sugar, along with the zest of ½ lemon and 1 tsp. ginger. It works best to cream the ginger and zest into the hazelnut butter.
3. Roll rectangle tightly and pinch at the seams. Cut into four 3-inch rolls and flatten the rolls with the heal of your hand.
4. Cut 3 notches along the length of each roll, being careful not to cut through the roll.
5. Place rolls on a greased baking sheet and lightly twist the cuts in a decorative fan.
6. Lightly mist rolls with water and allow them to rise until doubled. Preheat oven to 350°F.
7. Bake rolls for 30–35 minutes.

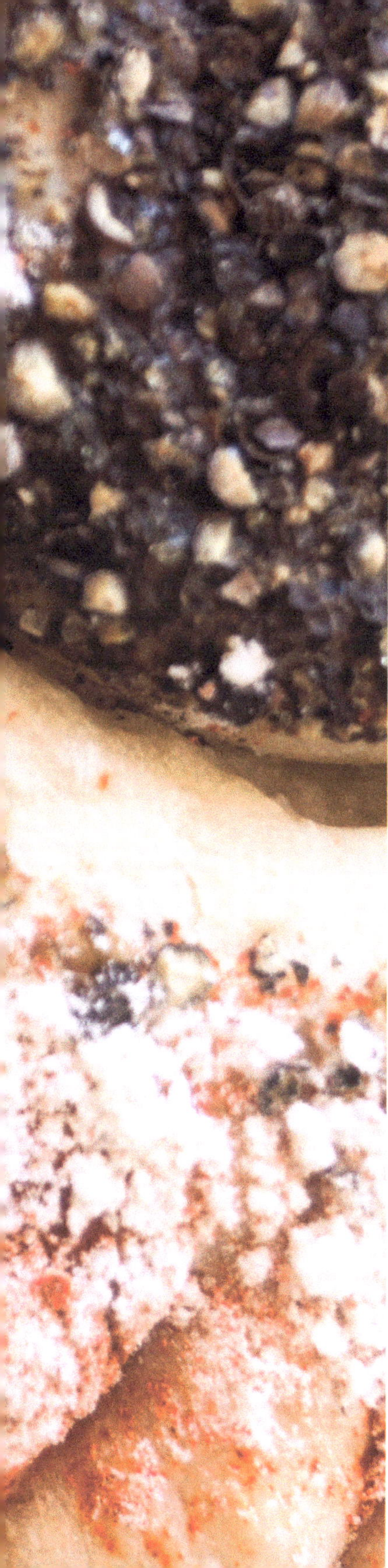

SPECIALTY DECORATIVE WREATHES & CROWN LOAVES

SUNFLOWER BREAD

Sunflower bread is probably one of my favorite decorative loaves. I am a complete dork for anything yellow, especially sunflowers. Looking at them makes me think of the 1970s. Maybe it's because I was smaller then, but I'm pretty sure everything I wore was covered in rickrack and paisley. This bread is covered in something better! I twist the petals in a delicious smoked paprika along with fresh cracked black pepper for the center of the flower. It not only has visual appeal, but it also doubles well as a pull-apart appetizer in the center of your dinner table.

TECHNIQUE:

1. Make 1 pound of bread dough from one of the simple bread recipes on page 11 (half of the Basic dough).
2. Roll out the dough in a circle ½ inch thick but small enough to fit on a full-size sheet pan (about 8 inches in diameter).
3. Transfer dough circle to a lightly oiled sheet pan or baking stone.
4. Place a small jelly jar in the center of the circle, lip side down. Lightly mist the top of the bread with water or flavored olive oil.
5. Sprinkle 1-2 tablespoons smoked paprika over the top of the dough without removing the jar. Lightly spread the paprika around, covering the dough that isn't hidden under the jelly jar.
6. Remove the jelly jar.
7. Cut ¾-inch wedges all the way around the circle, leaving the middle, where the jar had been, untouched.
8. Slightly pull out the wedges and lay them flat or twist them lightly before laying them flat for a more dramatic look.

TECHNIQUE CONTINUED ON NEXT PAGE

TECHNIQUE CONTINUED:

9. Mist the center of the flower with water and add fresh cracked black pepper.
10. Let dough rise until doubled.
11. Preheat oven to 375°F.
12. Bake for 30–35 minutes.
13. Serve sunflower warm with melted garlic butter for dipping.

CROWN LOAF

The crown loaf is a lot simpler to make than it appears. It makes a dramatic centerpiece on a holiday buffet table or an especially beautiful touch at a baptism or baby christening party. I am very fond of the look of any of the dark bread doughs (Simple Bread Recipes section) for this loaf, which appear natural and earthy like a grapevine wreath. In spite of the name, try not to wear it on your head to the next festival you attend. You'd look like an idiot.

TECHNIQUE:

1. Make 1 pound of bread dough from one of the simple bread recipes on page 11 (half of the Basic dough).

2. Roll out the dough in a circle ½ inch thick but small enough to fit on a full-size sheet pan (about 8 inches in diameter).

3. Cut a small *X* in the center of the circle and pinch the outside edges of the dough in a rolling motion toward the center. When you get the outside edge rolled to the center, pinch the seam tightly.

4. Turn the loaf over so the smooth side is up. Press lightly all the way around.

5. Cut the outside edge of the loaf with slits about 1 inch deep and 2 inches apart. Cut a second slit about ½ inch away from the first slit, all the way around at all the marks.

6. Pull the dough tabs out all the way around the loaf and roll into "fingers" attached to the loaf.

7. Twist the dough fingers into rosettes and place on the larger sections of the crown.

8. Transfer the crown to an oiled 12-inch (or larger) baking stone or baking sheet.

9. Allow the dough to rise until doubled in size.

TECHNIQUE CONTINUED ON NEXT PAGE

TECHNIQUE CONTINUED:

10. Preheat oven to 400°F.

11. Bake for 30–35 minutes (until 165°F internal temperature).

12. Remove crown loaf from oven and allow to cool.

DOUGH EMBELLISHMENTS:

If desired, attach decorative dough embellishments by misting the loaf with water and attaching embellishments. Return to oven and bake at 350°F until dough is cooked crisp. Paint with edible decorative paint if desired.

EDIBLE FLOWER EMBELLISHMENTS

Now that I've given you the recipe for the simple decorative dough embellishments (p. 49), I'll show you how to use it for floral design. I love how whole grain speckles the dough so when the bread is cooked it can either be painted in a decorative way or left au natural. I think the natural look is amazingly similar to all the ornate stone-carved cathedrals in Europe.

ROSES

TECHNIQUE:

1. Make one of the decorative dough recipes (p. 49). Roll a ball of decorative dough flat, to $^1/_{16}$-inch thickness, keeping the surface of the table lightly floured.
2. Cut several small circles equal size out of the thin decorative dough.
3. Stack 3 disks of dough.
4. Begin curling the dough toward the inside of the circle, being sure to catch the bottom overlapping disks of dough as you roll. This will start to form the rose.
5. Continue to roll, lightly pinching the center of the roll. Each side of the roll will look identical.
6. With your finger or a pencil, lightly dent the middle of the roll. Pinch the dough in the center until 2 roses separate.
7. Gently roll down the outer petals of the roses. Place them on a metal cooling rack to dry for a bit.
8. Use the roses on any decorative breads by lightly misting the top of the loaf with water just before baking. Indent the loaf with your thumb. Place the roses on top of the loaf inside your thumb indenture and bake. It is also possible to affix roses to already baked bread by misting the top of the prebaked loaf with water heavily and then lightly pressing the rose into the loaf. Mist the loaf and rose again with water and bake at 375°F for 10 more minutes. Remove from oven and allow to cool.

DAISIES

Daisies are made by using daisy cutters and stacking the dough. For decorative dough, use a chopstick or a sharp tool to seal the petals together.

TECHNIQUE:

1. Make any of the simple decorative dough embellishment recipes (p. 49). When the dough is rolled thin, cut the flowers from the dough with a daisy-shaped gum-paste cutter. Transfer daisies to a cooling rack, packing each flower a little into the mesh of the rack to create depth in the flower.

2. Put a small ball of dough in the center of each flower to finish it.

3. Mist each flower lightly with water, which will seal the flowers together.

4. Use the daisies on any decorative breads or rolls by lightly misting the top of the bread with water just before baking. (See the simple decorative dough embellishment tutorial on p. 50.) Indent the loaf with your thumb in an artistic pattern of your choice where you will place your flower. Place the daises on top of the loaf inside your thumb indenture and bake. Mist the loaf and flowers again with water and bake at 375°F for 10–15 minutes. Remove bread from oven and allow to cool.

CARNATIONS

Carnations are one of the simplest flowers to make. They are quick and add a fantastically dramatic appearance to your bread.

TECHNIQUE:

1. Make any of the simple decorative dough embellishment recipes (p. 49). When the dough is rolled thin, cut the dough into 1 inch by 2 inch strips. Lightly cut petal fringe into the entire length of each side of the strip, leaving ½ inch of uncut dough down the center.

2. Roll strips tightly down the center, leaving the flower petal fringe untouched.

3. Divide each strip into 2 flowers. Roll the petals down slightly.

4. Use the carnations on any decorative breads or rolls by lightly misting the top of the bread with water just before baking. (See the simple decorative dough embellishment tutorial on p. 50.) Indent the loaf with your thumb in an artistic pattern of your choice where you will place your flowers. Place the flowers on top of the loaf inside your thumb indenture and bake. Mist the loaf and flowers again with water and bake at 375°F for 10–15 minutes. Remove bread from oven and allow to cool.

LEAVES & VINES

Often the most dramatic look on a loaf of bread is the simple addition of some leaves or vines. They have universal appeal. Attach them to your bread and maybe Romeo will climb up the vines outside your bedroom window and carry you away. If Romeo does show up, give him some of your beautiful bread. He'll be swooning.

LEAF TECHNIQUE:

1. Make any of the simple decorative dough embellishment recipes (p. 49). Roll out dough paper thin.
2. Cut leaves out of the dough using either a gum-paste cutting tool or cut free-hand with a sharp knife.
3. Make knife marks at the veins of the leaves and pinch the leaf a little for added realistic depth.
4. Place the leaves on a drying rack.
5. Mist the surface of a light-colored baked bread (see simple bread recipes, p. 11) with water.
6. Lightly press the leaves into the surface of the loaf. Mist again with water.
7. Bake in a 350-degree oven until crisp, about 15 minutes.

VINE TECHNIQUE:

1. Make any of the simple decorative dough embellishment recipes (p. 49). Roll out dough to about $^1/_{16}$-inch thickness.
2. Cut pieces of dough into strips. The thickness depends on how thick you want the vines.
3. Roll dough strips gently to make edges smooth.
4. Mist the surface of a light-colored baked bread (see simple bread recipes, p. 11) with a heavy spray of water.

5. Lightly press the vines onto the surface of the loaf. Mist again with water.

6. Bake in a 350°F oven until crisp, about 15 minutes.

NATURAL COLORS & EXTRACTS TIPS

TIPS FOR SUCCESS

- Use food-grade paintbrushes designed for cake decorating. These have fine hairs and will give a very refined look to your painting techniques.
- Clean your brushes between uses so that there isn't any transfer of bacteria and unwanted flavors or colors from one loaf to the next.
- For edible loaves, always use food-grade colorings and flavorings. The use of craft paint on bread is not recommended.
- Plan your design ahead of time or use food-grade stencils and stamps when painting. Once the design is applied, it is difficult to change it.
- Be creative but also keep it simple and elegant.
- Dark food colors with a black, blue, or red base tend to have a bitter undertone in their flavors. The over-use of these colors will adversely affect the flavor of your bread.

BREAD PAINTING WITH NATURAL COLORS & EXTRACTS

BROWNS: USING A GRAIN REDUCTION OF WHEAT OR BARLEY

INGREDIENTS:

1 cup whole grain wheat or barley

1–2 cups water

1 egg, yolk and white separated

1. Put the dry whole grain wheat or barley in a frying pan. Toast it until it is almost black.
2. Add the water and steep the grain for about 15 minutes. Strain the grain, reserving the liquid.
3. Return the liquid to the stove and continue to reduce until it's in a concentrated form.
4. Bake your loaf from any of the simple bread recipes (p. 11), just until it reaches an internal temperature of 165°F. After it's baked, keep your oven at 350 degrees.
5. Mix a small amount of the egg yolk with the concentrate. The more you add, the lighter the color will be on your bread. Keep a darker and lighter shade for contrasting colors. Also, have a container with just egg yolk.

PAINTING THE BREAD:

1. With a new paintbrush, make your initial design with the lighter color. Then return the loaf of bread to the oven for 5 minutes.
2. Remove loaf from the oven and paint with your darker color (and a clean paintbrush) for contrast and details.
3. Use the egg yolk for the lightest areas that you still want to have a little color.
4. Return the bread to the oven and bake for an additional 5 minutes. This will set the color.
5. Remove the bread from the oven and lightly brush with the egg white.
6. Return to the oven again for a final 5 minutes.

BROWNS: USING ESPRESSO POWDER OR POWDERED GRAIN DRINK

This is my preferred technique for making the natural brown colors on my loaves. Bake any of the basic bread recipes (p. 11).

Dissolve 2–3 tablespoons espresso powder or powdered grain drink (like Pero or Cafix) with 1–2 teaspoons very hot water until a paint consistency is formed. It should be slightly thick but not a paste.

Paint the baked loaf lightly with the mixture in decorative swirls or designs as desired.

Return to the oven and bake at 350°F for 5 minutes to set the color.

USING BERRIES

My favorite berries for coloring the surface of loaves are blueberries. The natural juices are a bright lavender. Gently squeeze the berry between your fingers onto your paintbrush, or you can use the juice of several berries. Allow the paint to air-dry on the surface of the loaf. If you want a darker color, simmer the berries in a saucepan over low heat until the juices evaporate slightly and a syrup is formed. This will give you a good dark red or pink. Blackberries are a great choice for making dark purple. Cactus fruit from a prickly pear cactus will give you a very bright pink (always wear gloves when working with cactus fruit because it stains excessively).

NATURAL YELLOW HUES WITH TURMERIC

A bold yellow color on the surface of your loaves can easily be achieved by making a thin paste out of natural ground turmeric or any curry powder. Add a little water to the spice and mix it with a brush until the desired consistency is achieved. Keep in mind that there is generally a strong flavor associated with turmeric and curry, so use a light hand whenever possible.

NATURAL ORANGE AND RED TONES WITH ANNATTO

Annatto is a spice often used in Mexican and Spanish cooking to flavor rice dishes and soups. It is also used a lot in the food industry to color orange cheese crackers and dairy products. You can find ground annatto in most grocery stores, but you may have to look in the international foods section of your local store. To make dark orange or red tones, add a small amount of water to your ground annatto and lightly brush your desired pattern onto your loaf. Allow to air-dry.

FOOD-GRADE COLORING, PEARLS, DUSTING & GLITTER

FOOD COLORING

Very often the easiest decorative medium is the dropper-style food coloring you can get at a regular grocery store in the baking aisle.

I like to use an ice cube tray without ice in it as a convenient place to add a few dots of color. Another option is a food-grade pill dispenser (like the ones that are made for the days of the week). The pill dispensers are great because each compartment will close tight and you won't end up wasting any of your food coloring between decorating projects. Or I will often use a cupcake liner as my paint holder. They are inexpensive and easy to use for mixing color.

Add a 1–2 teaspoons water, depending on how intense you want the color to turn out in your finished painting application.

Dark food colors such as blacks, blues, and reds tend to have a bitter undertone if used to excess on your surfaces. Use them strictly as an accent instead of the main decorative theme.

WHITE PAINTS

Edible white-on-white food-grade paint is made by a few of the cake decorating companies to add to buttercream frostings since they go ivory because of the use of real butter. This food-grade coloring is also the perfect white accent coloring for bread-painting techniques.

Paint your white accents on your loaf of bread when it is still warm—the white coloring will tend to smudge excessively if done on cool bread.

GOLD, SILVER, AND AIRBRUSH COLOR: Manufacturers of cake decorating supplies make small cans of propellant gold, silver, and "airbrush" color sprays. These are excellent for the porous surfaces of bread, and the edible shimmer of these products will give you a dramatic effect when embellishing wedding, baby shower, or special holiday loaves. Use a light hand with these propellants because they are powerful in their ability to cover a lot of area quickly.

AIRBRUSH GELS: Similar in appearance to the small droppers of food coloring you can purchase at the grocery store, these little dropper tubes are available at most cake decorating and craft stores. Because of the concentration and consistency of these colors, they are optimum for bread decorating and come in a wide variety of colors. This becomes especially helpful when making a large number of matching rolls or loaves for a banquet instead of an isolated creation. When using the pearl and gold glazes, be sure to shake well before using. The pearl tends to settle to the bottom of the mixture.

PEARL DUSTING: This is available in gold, bronze, silver, pearl, rose, and green. The addition of a light dusting of edible pearl powder can add an isolated shimmer to any of your flowers or decorative dough touches. These edible pearl dusts are a bit on the expensive side, so use them sparingly. For a light color, gently fluff the brush with pearl dust onto your bread. For a more dramatic effect, dip your decorative paintbrush into a little water and use the pearl dust as you would paint. Some of my most dramatic loaves are made by a small and simple decorative swirl of a brush loaded with a pearl dust. It is sheer, simple, and elegant.

STENCIL TECHNIQUES

The use of a food-grade stencil is perhaps the simplest and yet most effective way to employ the bread-painting techniques (p. 113) in large number. The design is consistently beautiful and easy to duplicate, making it ideal for large luncheons and banquets when an especially simple yet elegant effect is desired. If you are having a hard time finding food-grade stencils, you can find a list of sources at the end of this book.

LEAVES & VINES WITH LARGER STENCILS

A few years back, I was contacted by a sweet woman named Kathy Peterson. She's a lifestyle and design expert in Florida and has been nationally known for her work for many years. We spoke on the phone about crafts, art, and creativity. She encouraged me to write this book. Kathy became a mentor to me in the field of craft and art design, and I'm happy to call her my friend. Kathy Peterson (www.kathypeterson.com) can often be seen on Lifetime for Women. She has a full line of food-grade stencils that can be used for bread and for walls in your home. I called her company myself to be sure, and they confirmed that the stencils are okay to use with food! I was thrilled to find that this leaf and vine stencil could be used on a loaf of prebaked ciabatta bread for a very dramatic effect.

TECHNIQUE:

1. Obtain a loaf of prebaked ciabatta bread approximately 1 foot long by 8 inches wide (or bake your own).
2. Wrap the stencil around your loaf, keeping it tight enough to the loaf that it doesn't slip.
3. With a fine-tipped food-grade paintbrush, lightly brush the color on the surface of the loaf between the openings of the stencil. Continue until the full design is filled in on the surface of your loaf.
4. Remove stencil.
5. Set color by placing the loaf in a preheated 350-degree oven for 5–10 minutes. Loaf will brown slightly and colors will set.
6. Glaze with edible gold or silver spray if desired.

STAMPING

Many cake decorating companies have come out with food-grade stamps that can be lightly coated with a thin layer of food coloring or natural colorings and stamped directly onto the surface of bread for bold and dramatic loaves. Look for different shapes and sizes to fit the theme of your breads, and be creative!

TECHNIQUE:

1. Lightly paint a stamp with food-grade paint or natural color of your choice (see bread-painting section, p. 113).
2. Press the stamp color side down onto the surface of your baked loaf or bun. Be careful not to press through the surface of the bread. Allow the color to air-dry. Repeat as desired with different colors.
3. Return loaf or bun to the oven to set the color, 375°F for 5 minutes.

LOAF-SEEDING TECHNIQUES

SEEDED BREAD

Unless you use a lot of denture cream, seeded bread is something that is really hard to resist! The addition of flavor, crunch, texture, and visual appeal is hard to beat, and it is a simple technique to master. Smack your lips together and give a cheer for seeds!

TECHNIQUE:

1. Make any of the simple bread recipes (p. 11) and follow the loaf-molding technique (p. 67) or roll-molding technique (p. 68). Once the loaf or rolls are formed, you will need ½ cup of your favorite seeds and a loaf pan or sheet pan (depending on the style of bread or rolls you desire). Make sure the pan is greased sufficiently.
2. Spread the seeds out on a clean work surface in a heavy coating.
3. Mist the loaf or rolls heavily with water.
4. Roll the bread in the seeds until coated. Transfer to the sheet pan or loaf pan.
5. Allow dough to rise until doubled in size.
6. Bake savory loaves at 425°F for 35–40 minutes. Bake rolls at 425°F for 15–18 minutes.
7. Remove bread from the oven and allow to cool. If you made a loaf, remove it from the pan and place on a cooling rack if desired.

PEPPER

USING SEEDS & GRAINS TO FIT YOUR BREAD THEME

STAR APPLIQUÉ LOAF
(*APPLIQUÉ TECHNIQUE ADDING SEEDS*)

With this particular loaf, and as a general rule, use seeds and embellishments that will complement the flavor of the loaf. Coarse ground sugar or salt can always be applied in a similar manner to the appliqué of dough, so have fun and be creative.

TECHNIQUE:

1. Obtain a 1-pound loaf of baked bread or any smaller rolls of your choice (see the simple bread recipes on p. 11). I love making this one with Basic White Bread (p. 27).
2. Carefully roll out a circle of any of the decorative dough recipes (p. 49) to 1/16 inch.
3. Mist the top of the loaf or bun with water.
4. Carefully cut out your desired shape from the decorative dough.
5. Lightly press the dough piece flush to the surface of the loaf.
6. Mist again with water. Sprinkle the loaf's appliqué pieces with a complementary seed of your choice.
7. Preheat oven to 350°F.
8. Place decorated loaf on a sheet pan and bake for 10–15 minutes, until embellishment dough is crisp and golden.

ATTACHING ROLLED GRAINS TO BREAD

The decorative application of rolled grain to your bread becomes especially beautiful as the loaf raises because inevitably the surface of the loaf is studded with gorgeous pieces of rolled grain. In loaves like this, I will most often use a very fine-tipped brush with a small bit of white paint to weave vines between the grains to look like an intricately woven canvas of leaves against a night sky.

TECHNIQUE:

1. Make any of the dark dough recipes in the simple bread recipes section—I prefer Double Chocolate Bread (p. 37). Follow the loaf-molding technique on page 67.
2. Once the loaf is formed, you will need ½ cup of your favorite rolled grain and a loaf pan or sheet pan (depending on the style of the bread you want to make). Make sure the pan is greased sufficiently.
3. Spread the rolled grain out on a clean work surface in a heavy coating.
4. Mist the loaf of bread heavily with water.
5. Roll the loaf in the grain until coated.
6. Transfer the loaf to the sheet pan or loaf pan.
7. Allow the loaf to rise until doubled in size.
8. Bake the loaf at 425°F for 35–40 minutes.
9. Remove the bread from the oven and allow to cool. If desired, remove the loaf from the pan and place on a cooling rack.
10. If desired, paint the bread with any of the decorative painting techniques of your choice.

ANIMAL BREADS

FISH

As with any work of art, having a living specimen or picture of a subject you wish to create is always helpful. There are thousands of different fish in the sea, and all of them can be used as the inspiration for your next decorative loaf.

TECHNIQUE:

1. Make 1 pound of dough or enough dough to make a single loaf of bread from any recipe in the simple bread recipes section (p. 11).
2. Form the body of the fish by rolling or folding the loaf into a long baguette, retaining a few lumps of dough for the creation of the fins. Taper one end of the baguette into a tail and pinch the other end into a mouth shape.
3. Place your formed loaf on a well-oiled full-sized sheet pan.
4. Roll out your fins as desired, keeping the dough ¼ inch thick. Tuck the fins underneath the body of the loaf and pinch. Lightly mist the loaf with a small amount of oil or water to keep the surface from drying too much.
5. Allow the dough to rise until about doubled in size, about 1 hour at room temperature, uncovered. Preheat oven to 400°F.
6. Bake for 30–35 minutes.
7. Remove the bread from the oven and allow cool.
8. Decorate with edible paints as desired.

RABBIT

Try not to read too much into the fact that I have a rabbit head decoratively displayed on a charger. I didn't kill the Easter Bunny because he brought me the wrong chocolate for my basket. Actually, most kids will think this is about the best thing you could make for a springtime party! The adults will get a good laugh out of it as well.

TECHNIQUE:

1. Make 1 pound of bread dough from one of the simple bread recipes (p. 11), or enough to make 1 standard-sized loaf of bread. I love Mom's 5-Day Bread (p. 21) for this one.
2. Roll the dough into a tight ball.
3. Place the dough on a lightly oiled sheet pan. Lightly mist the dough with water or oil to avoid letting the dough surfaces get too dry.
4. Allow the dough to rise until doubled in size.
5. When the bread is sufficiently raised, preheat oven to 425°F. Bake the bread for 30–35 minutes or until internal temperature reaches over 165°F.
6. Remove the bread from the oven and allow to cool. Reduce the oven temperature to 350°F.
7. Make the decorative dough of your choice (p. 49). Roll out this dough into a pair of long rabbit ears, approximately half the length of the head. Remember to roll thin pieces. You will also need to roll and cut out a nose. Mist the loaf heavily with water. Affix the pieces of decorative dough to the bread, being careful not to push through the crust. Mist the bread heavily with water again.
8. Return the bread to the oven and bake for 15–20 more minutes until the embellishments are crisp and golden.
9. Remove bread from the oven and allow to cool.
10. Paint the bread with decorative food coloring of your choice (see p. 113).

CALICO CAT APPLIQUÉ

The cat does not have your tongue, but he most certainly has your buns! This technique is like a decoupage . . . but with edible dough. I generally use a loaf of bread that is already baked, either homemade or store purchased. Look for lightly colored loaves for the best effect. This technique is simple enough in its application that even some of the most inexperienced bakers can do it. It doesn't have to be limited to cat cut-outs. Any piece of dough can be applied to a loaf of bread and baked on in this manner. It just so happened that when I was creating, I was thinking of a cat. Be adventurous! There's no limit to what you can do with this technique!

APPLIQUÉ TECHNIQUE:

1. Obtain a 1-pound loaf of baked bread or any smaller rolls of your choice. I use Basic White Bread (p. 27).
2. Make one of the decorative doughs (p. 49). Carefully roll out a 6-inch circle of the decorative doughs to $^{1}/_{16}$ inch.
3. Mist the top of the loaf or bun with water.
4. Carefully cut out your desired shape from the decorative dough circle.
5. Lightly press the dough piece flush to the surface of the loaf.
6. Mist the bread again with water.
7. Preheat the oven to 350°F.
8. Place the decorated loaf on a sheet pan and bake for 10–15 minutes until embellishment dough is crisp and golden.

BEAR BUNS

I have enjoyed these rolls since I was a child. They looked like little bear heads. I'd always eat the ears first. I have many fond memories of Christmas and other holidays with bear buns sitting on the kitchen table. Mom would take them to friends in a basket covered with a cloth, still warm. Then she'd ask the lucky recipient, "Do you want butter or jam on your bear buns?" If they had never had mom's buns, they'd usually laugh hysterically when she uncovered the buns. It was a lot of fun. Now you see where I get a bit of my zany food humor, right? Most often when I make bear buns, I will use two portions of the five-day bread dough (p. 21), but most bread dough will work for them. Chocolate yeast-raised dough, yeast-raised gingerbread, and even peasant rye dough will give you a dark brown bear. They're great for sandwiches and anytime you want a fun addition to your events. When my boys were in early grade school, I loved to put bear buns in their lunch boxes as a sweet surprise for their sandwiches.

TECHNIQUE:

1. For the dough, divide 1 recipe (for 2 loaves of bread) into 3 balls. This will yield 6 large bear buns or mini-loaves of bread.
2. Divide 2 of the balls into 3 balls (resulting in 6 balls).
3. Roll the 6 balls into buns and place on a stoneware pan lightly covered with cornmeal.
4. Divide the remaining ball in half. You will use this half for 12 ears.
5. Divide the other half into 6 balls, for the snouts. Attach the snouts and ears to the buns on the pan, pressing firmly into the buns.
6. Allow the buns on the stoneware pan to rise until almost doubled.
7. Add raisins or whole almonds to the buns for eyes and to the snouts for noses. Lightly mist the buns with water and allow them to sit for about 10 minutes while the oven preheats to 350°F.
8. Bake the buns for 30–35 minutes.
9. Ask the next person you see, "Do you want butter or jam on your bear buns?"

BIRD

There is a famous scene in the movie Mary Poppins where a sweet little old lady sits on a park bench and feeds hundreds of hungry pigeons with bags of bird feed. I think of that gal every single time I make bird bread. I bet she would have loved one of these to feed her birdies. With all the thousands of bird varieties in the world, the possibilities for this style of bread are endless.

TECHNIQUE:

1. Make 1 pound of dough or enough dough to make a single loaf of bread. I use Basic Sweet Bread (p. 24) most often.
2. Form the body of the bird by rolling or folding the dough into a long baguette, retaining a few lumps of dough for the creation of the feathers and beak.
3. Place your formed loaf on a well-oiled full-sized sheet pan.
4. Roll out your feathers and beak as desired, keeping the dough ¼ inch thick. Tuck the feathers underneath the body of the loaf and pinch. Lightly mist the loaf with a small amount of oil or water to keep the surface from drying too much.
5. Allow the dough to rise until about doubled in size, about 1 hour at room temperature, uncovered. Preheat oven to 400°F.
6. Bake for 30–35 minutes.
7. Remove bread from the oven and allow to cool.
8. Decorate the bread with edible paints as desired (see p. 113).

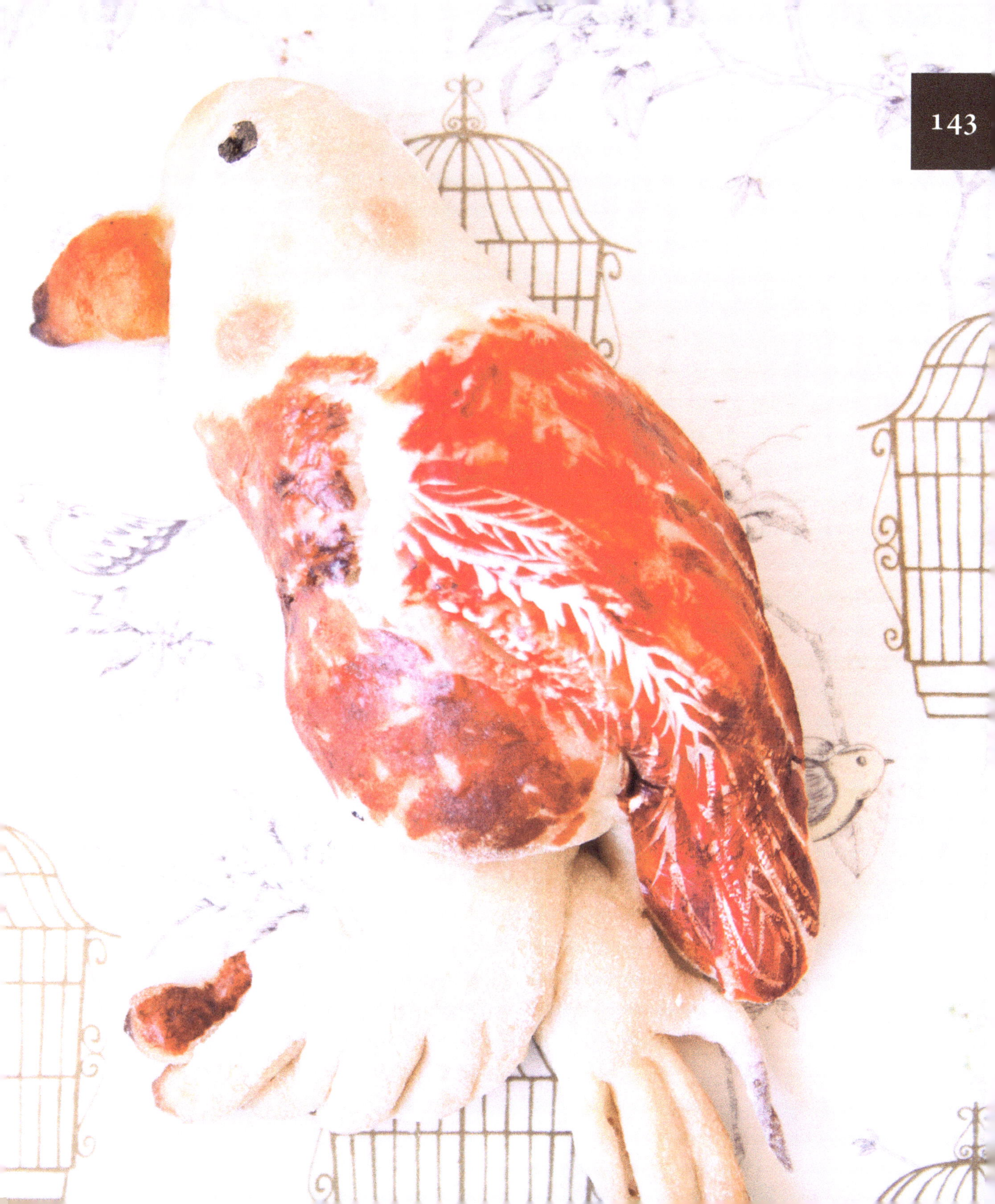

THEMED BREAD & BUNS

FALL TREE BREAD & FLOUR-DUSTED ARTISAN BREAD

How often do you see a loaf of artisan bread that is heavily dusted with flour? I see them in bake shops all over the country, and it always makes me want to paint. I don't know why. However, when I am being creative, the coating of flour is just the right medium to soak up the decorative edible paints and give the loaf a beautiful water-colored effect. Use your imagination the next time you see a loaf of artisan bread or bake one yourself! What about a winter snowflake motif? What about full-sized fall leaves or a bouquet of springtime hydrangeas?

TECHNIQUE:

1. Obtain a 1-pound loaf of flour-dusted artisan bread, or bake your own using any of the recipes outlined in the simple bread recipes section (p. 11). To dust a homemade loaf with flour, mist the top of the loaf with water after it has risen sufficiently to go in the oven and coat with ¼–½ cup fine-milled white flour. Slash the loaf with a sharp knife for decoration.

2. Bake the bread according to recipe directions.

3. When the loaf is baked through, remove it from the oven and allow it to cool. Pat off a little of the flour.

4. Use any of the decorative bread-painting techniques (p. 113) to apply colors, like a tree, to your loaf.

WEDDING LOAF FLOWER CLUSTERS

When preparing for a large buffet or event, this is the simplest technique for making several glamorous loaves at one time. It is done by either baking or obtaining many lightly colored loaves beforehand. You can make dough embellishments for the tops of the loaves up to a week ahead of your event if stored in the open air.

TECHNIQUE:

1. Premake as many flowers and leaves as desired using the edible decorative bread embellishment recipe of your choice (pp. 49 and 103). Make sure the flowers and leaves are rolled thin out of the dough.

2. Mist the top your loaf with water 24–48 hours before the event. Press the dough embellishments into the loaf, being careful not to push through the crust too harshly.

3. Mist the embellishments with water again. This will act as a glue, holding the pieces to the loaf. Preheat oven to 350°F.

4. Bake the loaf for 10–15 minutes, until golden brown.

5. Paint with decorative colors and pearl glazes as desired (see bread-painting section, p. 113).

SALTED SWEET SEASHELL BREAD

Any sweet bread with a sprinkle of sea salt is a wonderful combination, and I am particularly fond of this loaf of bread—made into the shape of a seashell and then baked on top of a little salt, which adds a unique texture. This loaf is painted with decorative edible brown paint to accent the shell appearance and misted with edible gold. It is absolutely stunning!

TECHNIQUE:

1. Make enough dough for 1 loaf of Basic Sweet Bread (p. 24) and roll it into a tight ball.
2. Oil a standard baking sheet and sprinkle the sheet with 1–2 tablespoons kosher sea salt.
3. Place the ball of dough onto the salt.
4. Cover the dough with a light mist of oil or water to avoid letting the surface of the bread dry out. Allow the dough to rise until doubled in size.
5. Preheat the oven to 425°F.
6. Bake for 35–40 minutes until lightly browned.
7. Remove the bread from the oven and allow to cool.
8. Paint the bread with a natural brown coloring (pp. 114–115).
9. Return the loaf to the oven to set color, about 5 minutes.
10. Allow the bread to cool again.
11. Lightly mist the bread with edible gold airbrush color (p. 119).

WEDDING OR BRIDAL SHOWER ROLLS

Perhaps my most reliable inspiration for decorative bread comes from designs I see applied to dishes that I'll be using at an event. The first time I fell in love with this particular method was looking at a cute yellow and white springtime salad bowl. I wanted to decorate my entire house with this pattern, but instead I opted for using it as the theme design for bridal shower rolls. The rolls looked absolutely adorable with a similar motif of the bowl, and the color of the rolls was already so similar to the golden-yellow of the bowl that I didn't have to match the color. You'll find inspiration in the most remarkable places. Create a stencil if you're making many rolls by drawing your design on a piece of light cardboard and then cutting it out with an X-Acto razor. Next time, I'm totally going to try to match someone's tattoo.

TECHNIQUE:

1. Find a pattern on a dish, bowl, or other inspirational piece. Decide how detailed you want your finished design.
2. Pick complementary colors to your dish and lightly paint your design onto your baked rolls using white-on-white edible paint (p. 117) mixed with the color you prefer.
3. Place rolls in the oven at 350°F for 5 more minutes to set the color. Do not overbake or the white will burn.

LILAC CLUSTERS (FLORAL DEPTH TECHNIQUE)

As a little girl, I could often be found under my grandmother's large lilac bush sniffing and drinking in the aroma of the beautiful purple blooms. I was a strange child. It is a wonder I never ended up with some of those blooms in my nostrils. The lilac bush has faded now, but whenever I think of home, I miss lilacs. It isn't a surprise that this is a common motif I use for dinner rolls. Use three or four different hues of purple to give the illusion of depth and keep the details more impressionistic than exact—this will add to the beauty of these rolls.

TECHNIQUE:

1. Prebake rolls (see simple bread recipes, p. 11). Use a prebaked hard dinner roll with a smooth surface for this particular style of decorating (see roll-molding tips on p. 68).
2. Combine 3 or 4 different hues of a color (see bread-painting section, p. 113). One should be very dark and one should be almost white, with two shades in between.
3. Apply a painted cluster of dark flowers.
4. Alternate your colors with the next hue of colored flowers, painting until you get to the lightest-colored flower.
5. Accent the flowers with leaves.
6. Lightly mist with pearl or gold edible airbrush color if desired.
7. To set the color, return bread to the oven, 375°F for 5 minutes.

VALENTINE'S HEART BUNS

Simple heartfelt sentiment is always preferable in my world. If you can add a delicate heart to a bun and do so in such a way that it stands alone in beauty, then you have achieved success.

TECHNIQUE:

1. Prebake rolls (see simple bread recipes, p. 11). I love to use Double Chocolate Bread for the rolls (p. 37). Use a prebaked hard dinner roll with a smooth surface for this particular style of decorating (see roll-molding tips, p. 68).
2. Apply a thin layer of white-on-white edible paint (p. 117) in the shape of a heart (see bread-painting section, p. 113).
3. Accent the heart with red swirls using a medium bristled brush.
4. Bake the rolls in a 350-degree oven for 5 minutes to set color.

FRENCH ROLLS

The fleur-de-lis is the French stylized lily or iris that is used for decorative designs. I love putting it on hard French rolls in a gorgeous red or more natural brown. I'd probably have used this on rolls for the Cub Scout blue-and-gold banquet if I really thought my sons would have appreciated the extra work. As it is, I reserve these for my lady friends. Use a handmade or store-purchased stencil for larger gatherings or bigger loaves of bread.

TECHNIQUE:

1. Bake rolls (see simple bread recipes, p. 11). I prefer to use rolls baked from the Basic White Bread dough (p. 27). Decide which size design you would like to apply to your particular rolls or bread.

2. Create a stencil or purchase a food-grade one.

3. With a handmade or store-bought food-grade stencil, lightly outline the fleur-de-lis with a fine-tipped brush dipped in a light color (see bread-painting techniques, p. 113, and stencil techniques, p. 121).

4. Fill in the details with a wider brush.

5. If using red, remember to thin out the color so that the flavor is not too bitter from the food coloring.

6. There's no need to rebake the loaves or rolls if using a food coloring.

INDIAN POTTERY LOAF

This bread-painting style has become particularly popular in the Arizona desert where I live. It is an earth-toned loaf with dark red and brown accents on hardy, crusty bread. I adore mimicking the angles and styles of the petrographs of Native Americans. I serve this with a thick spicy stew on a cold night.

TECHNIQUE:

1. Make dough for 1 loaf of bread from any of the simple bread recipes (p. 11).
2. Grease a heavy-bottomed sheet pan or pizza stone (18 inches or longer).
3. Lightly flour a countertop and roll the dough out in a 14-inch rectangle. Roll it in a tight log, pinching the seams together firmly.
4. Place the log seam side down on the baking sheet.
5. Allow the dough to rise uncovered and un-oiled until almost tripled in size, about 2 hours.
6. Preheat the oven to 450°F. Mist the top of the bread with water. With a sharp serrated knife, lightly slit a straight line down the entire length of the loaf.
7. Bake the bread for 20–25 minutes (until 165°F internal temperature).
8. Remove the bread from the oven and allow to cool. Reduce the heat in the oven to 350°F.
9. While the loaf is still hot, paint it with brown and red hues (see bread-painting section, p. 113) in a southwestern pattern or design of your choice.
10. Return the loaf to the oven for 3–5 more minutes to set the color.

POLKA-DOT BUNS

Can I kiss the person who invented the polka dot? I've loved the simple and fun appearance of the dot on so many of my dishes, clothing, and linens that I'm pretty sure I have an addiction. If there's a program for overcoming the compulsion to add dots to everything, I'll never go to a meeting. Dots don't make you fat. Dots don't compare themselves to you. Dots don't snore. They're just fun little friends who keep things light and delightful. Okay, I admit it, now I'm starting to sound like I really have a problem. Dot-obsessive freaks unite! This bun is for you.

TECHNIQUE:

1. Obtain a dozen hard rolls with a very smooth crust or bake them yourself. I prefer Mom's Five-Day Bread (p. 21).
2. Use the bread-painting technique of your choice to apply dots (see p. 113).
3. Apply more dots. Apply bigger dots. Apply contrasting dots. Add some stripes. Add more dots. Look for a 12-step program—you're addicted.

RED & BLACK MINI BAGUETTES

If Cruella de Vil was hosting a party and she couldn't have fur on her finger-food, I bet she'd do the next best thing and serve these charming and whimsical buns. Serve them at your next luncheon and watch the astonishment and pleasure of your friends. Your guests might not want to eat them because they're too cute.

TECHNIQUE:

1. Make enough dough for 1 loaf, using the recipe for Basic White Bread (p. 27) or Mom's Five-Day Bread (p. 21). Divide the dough into 6 pieces. Roll each piece into a tight log (about 4 inches long), pinching the seams tightly together.
2. Place the baguettes 2 inches apart on a greased sheet pan.
3. Allow the dough to rise until doubled in size, uncovered, 1–1½ hours.
4. Preheat the oven to 450°F and mist the top of the bread with a heavy coat of water.
5. Bake the bread for 16–18 minutes (until 165°F internal temperature).
6. Remove the bread from the oven and allow it to cool. Reduce the temperature of the oven to 350°F.
7. Decorate the surface of the bread with thin-rolled decorative dough embellishments (Rye on p. 58 or Oat on p. 57) by misting the surface with water and gently pressing the pieces into the loaf.
8. Mist the bread again with water and return to the oven. Bake for an additional 10–12 minutes, until golden.
9. Remove the bread from the oven and paint with red and black embellishments (see bread-painting section, p. 113).

FANCY BAGUETTES

FRESH HERB BAGUETTE

Perhaps the most natural of all the loaves I make is this herb loaf, embellished with natural leaves from fresh edible plants. It is delightful to look at and even more delicious to eat. The secret is using egg white as the glue to get the herbs to stick to the surface of the bread. This technique can be used with either bread you bake yourself or bread purchased at a local bakery. And it can also be used with dinner rolls and edible culinary flowers like pansies, carnations, and roses. If you opt for fresh flowers, be sure they are organic and have never been exposed to pesticides. You don't want toxic chemicals on your bread.

TECHNIQUE:

1. Obtain a baguette of light-colored bread that is slightly underbaked, or bake your own baguette using any of the simple bread recipes (p. 11). I love using Basic White Bread (p. 27).

2. Once the baguette is baked, crack a single egg in half and separate the white. With a food-grade paintbrush, gently apply a thin coat of egg white to the surface of the bread where you would like to affix a fresh herb leaf or flower. Press the leaf onto the egg white and hold for several seconds until the leaf stays attached. Repeat this process until the loaf is embellished as desired.

3. Once the leaves are attached, preheat the oven to 325°F. Lightly paint over the leaves one more time with a coating of egg white, being careful not to let the egg pool too much on the surface of the bread. Place the bread on a sheet pan and bake for 10–12 minutes until egg is dried.

4. Remove the bread from the oven and apply any decorative bread-painting techniques you desire (see p. 113).

RYE FLORAL BAGUETTE

A long white French baguette embellished with natural dark roses and flowers can be done simply. Most local bakeshops make some version of French bread that can be used for this technique. When looking at loaves, try to find ones that have a slightly less dramatic slashing on the top of the loaf. This ensures there is enough space for your embellishments. Look for loaves that are pale in color. Using this technique with prebaked bread saves a lot of time and energy, but you still end up looking like a genius. I won't tell anyone your secret, but if anyone asks how you did it, I hope you share a copy of this book with them! Was that a shameless personal plug or what?

TECHNIQUE:

1. Obtain a baguette of light-colored bread that is slightly underbaked, or bake your own baguette using any of the simple bread recipes (p. 11). I love using Basic White Bread (p. 27).
2. Make a batch of Rye Decorative Dough (p. 58).
3. Lightly flour a tabletop. Keep the dough that is not being worked in a covered container. You can use cutting tools for ornate decorative bread dough.
4. Roll a ball of dough flat to 1/16-inch thickness, keeping the surface of the table lightly floured.
5. Cut out desired shapes and create roses and flowers using the techniques outlined in the edible flower embellishments section (p. 103).
6. Place the baked bread on a lightly oiled sheet pan.
7. Preheat oven to 350°F.
8. Mist the top of the loaf with a heavy coat of water. Carefully arrange the embellishments on the top of the loaf according to your preference. Mist the loaf heavily with water again.
9. Place the loaf in the preheated oven on the center rack and allow it to cook for 15–20 more minutes until the loaf is golden brown and the embellishments are crispy.

SPECIALTY PRODUCT SUPPLIERS

The following is a list of sources that I use for some of the specialty flours and products mentioned in this book. It's a short list but a good one to know.

FLOURS AND GRAINS

Honeyville Grain: I'm partial to Honeyville because I am their corporate chef and am familiar with the excellent quality they have in cleanliness and consistency. I've used all their bulk whole grains, flours, and grain mills. They have four retail stores on the West Coast of the United States and ship anywhere in the country from their online store for a low, flat rate.

www.honeyville.com

Toll-free: (888) 810-3212
Email: webmaster@honeyvillegrain.com

King Arthur Flour is an excellent resource for baking flours and supplies like baking pans.

www.kingarthurflour.com

(800) 827-683
Email: customercare@kingarthurflour.com

Kamut International is the best non-GMO, organic, whole-grain, high-protein grain source.

www.kamut.com

Unites States:
Montana Flours and Grains:
2500 Chouteau Street
P.O. Box 517
Fort Benton, Montana 59442

www.montanaflour.com

Bob's Red Mill: This is a great source for smaller bags of specialty grain and flours.

www.bobsredmill.com

United States:
5000 SE International Way
Milwaukie, OR 97222
(503) 607-6455

CHEF TESS SPICE BLENDS

Honeyville Grain: Honeyville private labels my spice blends, which are available online or in any of their four retail stores. They ship anywhere in the country from their online store for a low, flat rate.

www.honeyville.com

Toll-free: (888) 810-3212
Email: webmaster@honeyvillegrain.com

FOOD-GRADE STENCILS

Kathy Peterson: In this book I have used Kathy Peterson's stencils for many of the decorative designs. She has inspired me immensely! You can find out more from her website:

www.kathypeterson.com

Cutting Edge Stencils is the company that produces Kathy Peterson's stencils. They can be found here:

www.cuttingedgestencils.com/kathy-peterson-inspired.html

CUTTING TOOLS, FOOD COLORING, AND FOOD-GRADE PAINT BRUSHES

Wilton cake decorating supplies: These tools can be found in most craft and specialty cake decorating stores all over the United States.

www.wilton.com
Call (888) 373-4588 to place an order by phone

Wilton Industries
2240 W. 75th St. Woodridge, IL 60517
Phone: (800) 794-5866
Fax: (630) 963-7196 or (888) 824-9520

INDEX

G

H

I

K

L

M

N

O

P

R

Measurement Equivalents

Cups	Tablespoons	Fluid Ounces
⅛ cup	2 Tbsp.	1 fl. oz.
¼ cup	4 Tbsp.	2 fl. oz.
⅓ cup	5 Tbsp. + 1 tsp.	
½ cup	8 Tbsp.	4 fl. oz.
⅔ cup	10 Tbsp. + 2 tsp.	
¾ cup	12 Tbsp.	6 fl. oz.
1 cup	16 Tbsp.	8 fl. oz.

Cups	Fluid Ounces	Pints/Quarts/Gallons
1 cup	8 fl. oz.	½ pint
2 cups	16 fl. oz.	1 pint = ½ quart
3 cups	24 fl. oz.	1½ pints
4 cups	32 fl. oz.	2 pints = 1 quart
8 cups	64 fl. oz.	2 quarts = ½ gallon
16 cups	128 fl. oz.	4 quarts = 1 gallon

Other Helpful Equivalents

1 Tbsp	3 tsp.
8 oz.	½ lb.
16 oz.	1 lb.

Metric Measurement Equivalents

Approximate Weight Equivalents

Ounces	Pounds	Grams
4 oz.	¼ lb.	113 g
5 oz.		142 g
6 oz.		170 g
8 oz.	½ lb.	227 g
9 oz.		255 g
12 oz.	¾ lb.	340 g
16 oz.	1 lb.	454 g

Approximate Volume Equivalents

Cups	US Fluid Ounces	Milliliters
⅛ cup	1 fl. oz.	30 ml
¼ cup	2 fl. oz.	59 ml
½ cup	4 fl. oz.	118 ml
¾ cup	6 fl. oz.	177 ml
1 cup	8 fl. oz.	237 ml

Other Helpful Equivalents

½ tsp.	2½ ml
1 tsp.	5 ml
1 Tbsp.	15 ml

ABOUT THE AUTHOR

Chef Stephanie Petersen, also known as Chef Tess Bakeresse, is a full-time corporate chef and cooking instructor in Phoenix, Arizona. Stephanie is classically trained in pastry, having graduated from Scottsdale Culinary Institute (Arizona) in 1995. Stephanie is famous for her energy of spirit and bubbly personality. She worked in resort bakeshops as an assistant banquet chef and as a fruit and vegetable display artist. When she became a mother fifteen years ago, she set aside her work in the restaurant industry and focused full-time on her children.

Driven by a passion to create, she continued baking decorative edible breads for private events. To any mother with young children, the need to do something creative is very real. At the urging of a dear friend, she started a food blog called *Chef Tess Bakeresse.* Within six months of starting her blog, Stephanie was published internationally in *Australian Baking Business* magazine for her bread artistry. She was propelled toward a career in bread art and instruction. Stephanie has taught large group and personal cooking instruction for the last eight years. For the last four years, Stephanie has been a frequent TV guest chef and "idea extraordinaire" in Arizona and Utah with a national following. She also enjoys frequent visits to the local radio stations to participate in weekly radio shows.

Her passion for art and food make an amazing impact on all who have come to know her work. She is in every way a down-to-earth gal who adores teaching with a lighthearted whit, laughing, loving, and connecting with new people every day. She lives in Phoenix, Arizona, with her husband and two children and is very involved in church and community. In her free time she can be found curled up with a good cookbook, baking with her children, going on long walks in the desert, and singing.

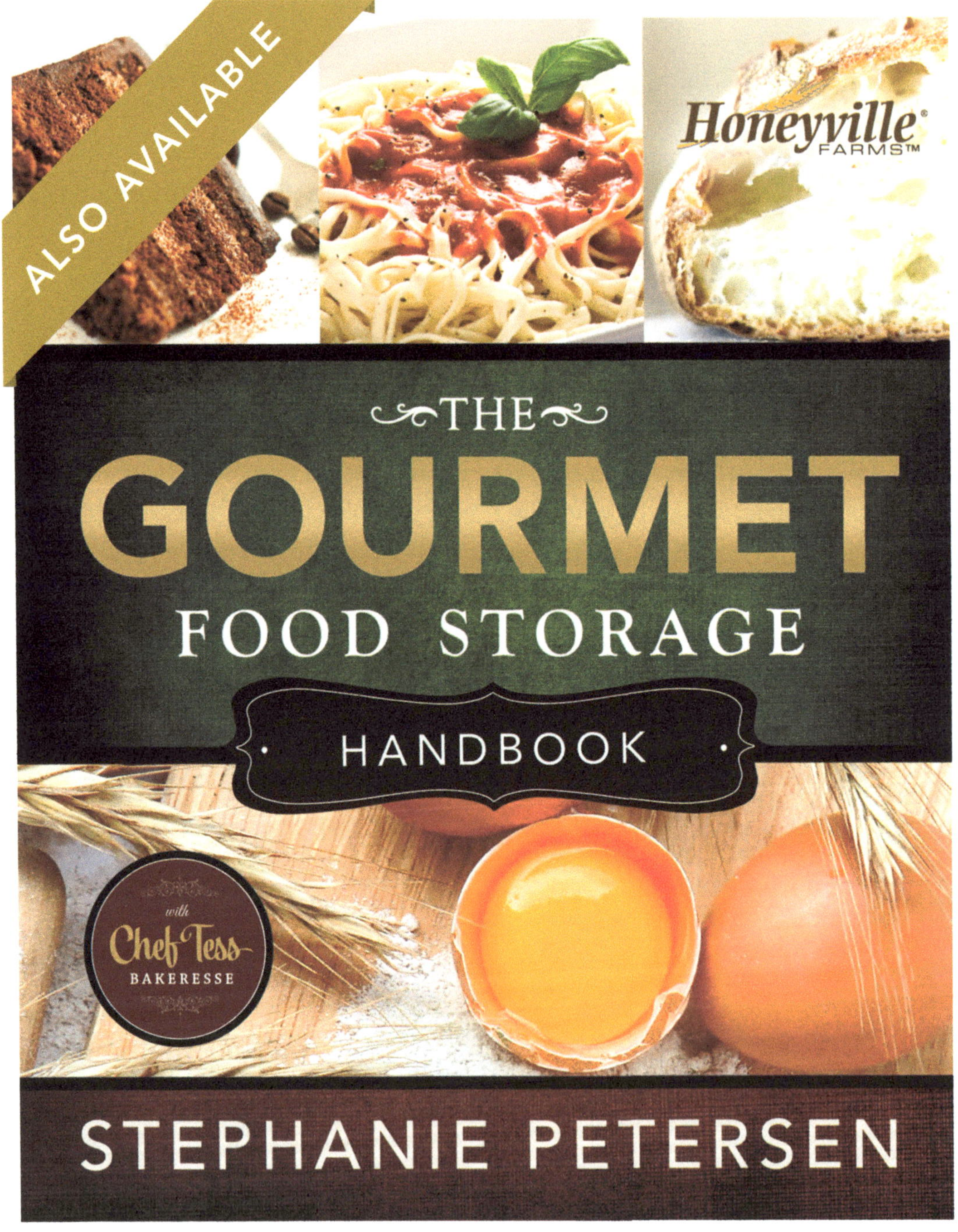
ALSO AVAILABLE
Honeyville
FARMS™
THE
GOURMET
FOOD STORAGE
HANDBOOK
with
Chef Tess
BAKERESSE
STEPHANIE PETERSEN

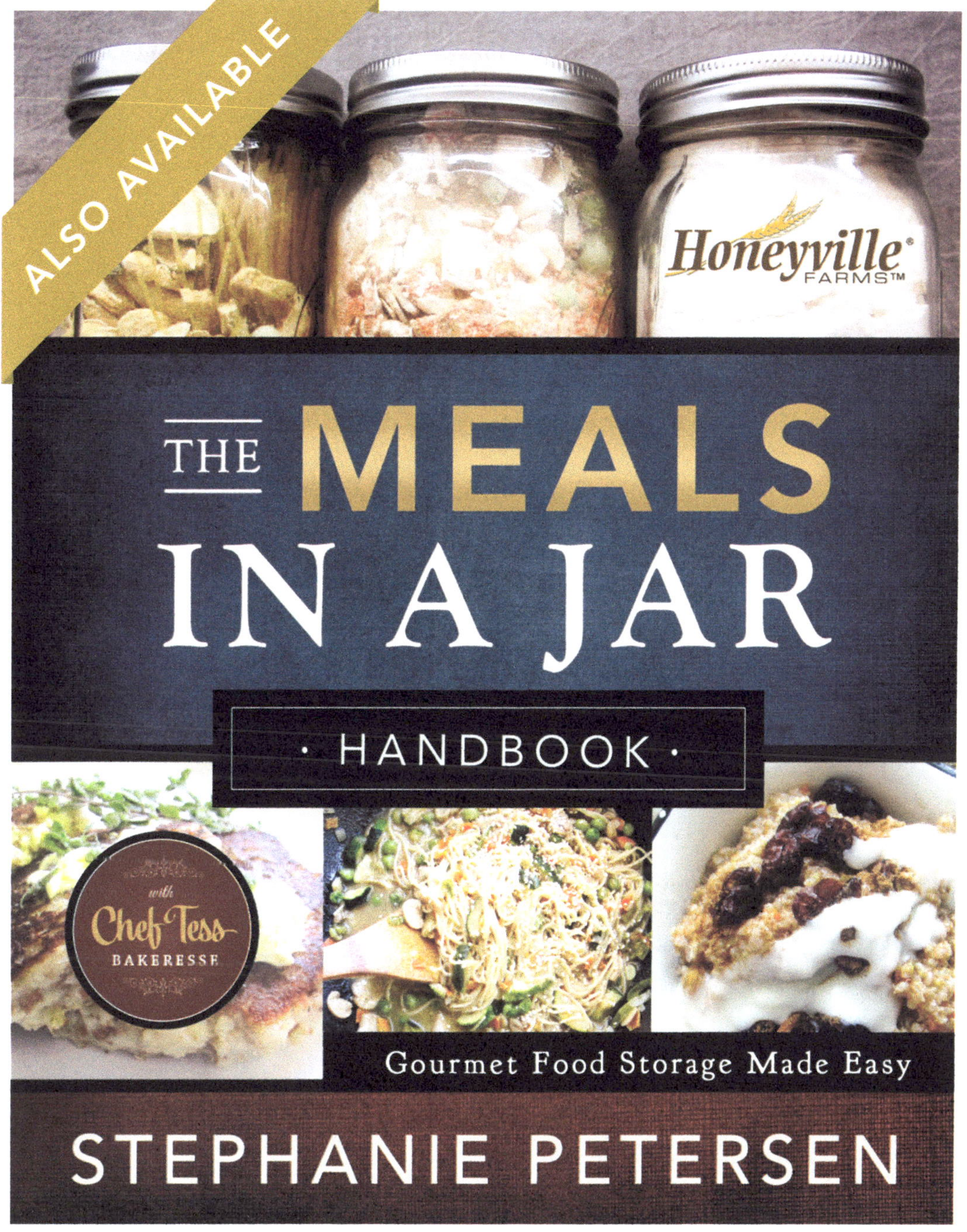
ALSO AVAILABLE
Honeyville FARMS
THE MEALS IN A JAR
· HANDBOOK ·
with Chef Tess BAKERESSE
Gourmet Food Storage Made Easy
STEPHANIE PETERSEN

0 26575 12951 9